HOW TO BE A MATURE CHRISTIAN

THE WISDOM OF THE BOOK OF JAMES
BY MARILYN HICKEY

HOW TO BE A MATURE CHRISTIAN

THE WISDOM OF THE BOOK OF JAMES
BY MARILYN HICKEY

MARILYN HICKEY MINISTRIES
P.O. Box 17340 • Denver, Colorado 80217

Unless otherwise indicated,
all Scripture quotations are taken from
the *King James Version* of the Bible.

CONTENTS

Introduction

Close to Divinity—Short of the Mark

To his congregation at the church of Jerusalem, James was a pastor. To the disciples of Jesus, James was a founder of the early church and a man of wisdom. To the modern-day church, our primary identification of James is that he was the half-brother of our Lord, Jesus Christ:

> *"Is not this the carpenter's son? is not his mother called Mary? and his brethren, James, and Joses, and Simon, and Judas?" (Matthew 13:55).*
>
> *Is not this the carpenter, the son of Mary, the brother of James, and Joses, and of Judah, and Simon? and are not his sisters here with us?" (Mark 6:3a).*

The Greek word for "brethren" or "brother" in both of these passages means "of the same womb," proving that Mary, the mother of Jesus, was the physical mother of children who were born after Him. They were fathered by Joseph, while Jesus was virgin-born.

Many people read the book of James and think, "No wonder James had such profound knowledge of God's Word. He had a special advantage because he grew up in the same household as Jesus!"

If only that were the case. Although James and Jesus were physically half-brothers, they were not initially spiritual brothers. In fact, at first James had no perception of who his brother was! Since during the Lord's earthly ministry His brothers and sisters still did not seem to understand who He really was, He did not call them His "brothers and sisters." Take, for example, the time when Jesus' family sought Him while He taught in a house near Jerusalem:

> *"And the multitude sat about him, and they said unto him, Behold, thy mother and thy brethren without seek for thee. And he answered them, saying, Who is my mother, or my brethren? And he looked round about on them which sat about him, and said, Behold my mother and my brethren! For whosoever shall do the will of God, the same is my brother, and my sister, and mother"* *(Mark 3:32-35).*

Imagine James' shock upon hearing this statement from Jesus! To the Lord, being physically related was not the most important thing. Since James was not a spiritual brother, Jesus did not consider him to be a brother at all. Rather, those sitting inside eager to learn God's Word were the Lord's brothers. You can be on the "inside" with an attitude of desiring to learn, or you can be on the "outside," watching with a critical eye. Your attitude will determine whether you are a brother to the Lord or not.

James did not believe in Jesus during His earthly ministry, and many times he found his brother to be an offense. On the few occasions when James seemed to accept Jesus' ministry, selfish motives lay behind the acceptance. One time James and his siblings surrounded the Lord before the Feast of Tabernacles and said, "Do a miracle at the Feast of Tabernacles! Let everyone see how great our brother really is. "

> *"His brethren therefore said unto him, Depart hence, and go into Judea, that thy disciples also may see the works that thou doest. For there is no man that doeth any thing in secret, and he himself seeketh to be known openly. If thou do these things, shew thyself to the world. For neither did his brethren believe in him" (John 7:3-5).*

Being related to Jesus was apparently no advantage to James and his family! At times, they had a total lack of spiritual discernment.

Many times we, as new Christians, feel hurt when our own relatives don't come into God's family right away. We wonder, "What's wrong with them? Don't they understand how important this is?"

If you were like many new believers, directly after you received the new birth you ran home and tried to convert your whole family in one hour. Occasionally this works for some people, but it's more often the exception than the rule. Attacking our families with the sword of the Spirit is seldom the way to win them! Sometimes, in our spirit of new zeal, we do more harm than good.

It is important for new believers to share the miracle of their new lives in Christ with relatives. But after sharing our good news, sometimes it's best to back off, love them, trust God for their salvation and pray for laborers to come to them. In most cases, pressure is a tactic to be left alone.

Jesus never pushed His relatives into salvation. He

never berated them for their unbelief. Jesus knew His purpose here on earth was to perform the Father's will by providing our salvation. He didn't get sidetracked into cares and worries, even by His own family. I believe He prayed for His loved ones to be saved. But He didn't have to pressure them. He knew it was God's will to save them.

It's the same way with you and me. If we commit ourselves to doing the will of God while we're here on earth, and pray for our loved ones, God will open the doors for their salavation. The door, for Jesus' brother, did not open until after the Lord's death and resurrection. Then a mighty miracle took place, and the life of James was never to be the same:

> *"Christ died for our sins according to the scriptures; And that he was buried, and that he rose again the third day according to the scriptures: And that he was seen of Cephas, then of the twelve: After that, he was seen of above five hundred brethren at once; of whom the greater part remain unto this present, but some are fallen asleep. After that, he was seen of James"* *(1 Corinthians 15:3b-7a).*

The Bible is silent on James' reaction to seeing the resurrected Christ. But it is clear that his stony heart was transformed into a heart of flesh—a heart prepared to receive the Word of God and then share it with others. On the day of Pentecost, the spiritual and physical family of Jesus were together in an Upper Room:

> *"And when they were come in, they went up into an upper room, where abode both Peter, and James, and John, and Andrew, Philip, and*

*Thomas, Bartholomew, and Matthew, James the
son of Alphaeus, and Simon Zelotes, and Judas
the brother of James. These all continued with
one accord in prayer and supplication, with the
women, and Mary, the mother of Jesus and with
his brethren" (Acts 1:13,14).*

Mary and her sons, among whom was James, were in
the first 120 people to receive the powerful baptism of
the Holy Spirit. You say, "How could James have
missed the Lord's earthly ministry? He performed so
many miracles!" James' eyes were blinded until after
the resurrection. Sometimes we can tell our loved ones
about the wonderful miracles taking place at our church,
yet their eyes are blinded also. How many of us heard
about Jesus hundreds of times—and then one day we
heard about Him "for the first time"? Our blindness
was dispelled, we fell in love with the Lord, and suddenly He was irresistible! That's how it was when the
light of the gospel finally shone in the hearts of James
and his family.

The Lord's family came around, and so will yours.
Don't give up on your loved ones. Your labor in the
Lord is never in vain.

New Nature, New Calling

James was no longer an outsider. He had become the
spiritual brother to the Lord: saved, baptized with the
Holy Spirit, and afire with the truth of God's Word. He
received a ministry gift to be a pastor and was a founder
of the church at Jerusalem.

I know that James had a pastor's sensitive heart
toward the Body of Christ. In his epistle the phrases,
"brethren," "my brethren," or "my beloved brethren"
appear 15 times!

As a church leader, James was skillful in understanding, living, and teaching God's Word. Every message in his book is based on the scripture. Because he practiced what he preached, his teachings were proven to be effective.

The disciples found James to be so full of wisdom and so reliable, they called on him to settle a major issue in the church—one that threatened to resurrect the old spirit of Jewish legalism, encumbering the freedom of grace by requiring new believers to be circumcised. In the city of Galatia, Paul called a conference and sent for James:

> *"But he, beckoning them with the hand to hold their peace, declared unto them how the Lord had brought him out of the prison. And he said, Go shew these things unto James, and to the brethren" (Acts 12:17a).*

Why was James' presence so important at this conference? This dispute needed to be resolved with the wisdom of God. James' wisdom is so highly recognized today that his epistle has been called "the Proverbs of the New Testament." James settled the heated arguments beautifully on the same day the disciples sent for him. How did he do it? By declaring the works of God:

> *"And the day following, Paul went in with us unto James; and all the elders were present. And when he had saluted them, he declared particularly what things God had wrought among the Gentiles by his ministry" (Acts 21:18,19).*

This book shares the wisdom of James with you. The theme of James' epistle is "Be mature as a Christian." That maturity comes one way: By practicing God's

Word, incorporating it into every facet of your life. James had seen Jesus and had become a true brother of Jesus. His book was written to help you walk as a mature brother of the Lord, just as he did.

Chapter One

HEAR THE WORD

During the Lord's earthly ministry, James had tried to provoke the Lord. It is a new James who opens his letter and identifies himself as, *"James, a servant of God and of the Lord Jesus Christ."* To James, there was no longer any calling higher than being a servant of God and His Son. That's maturity! James opens his letter:

"To the twelve tribes which are scattered abroad, greeting" (James 1:1b).

Throughout the Old Testament you can read how Israel's 12 tribes were scattered throughout the eastern world. First, 10 of the 12 tribes (called Israel) were taken into captivity by the nation of Assyria. The other two tribes (called Judah) were taken captive by the nation of Babylon. Later the Israelites were allowed to return home to rebuild their temple in Jerusalem. However, not all of them chose to return. Many of them would only return to Jerusalem to observe specific feast days.

Many of the practicing Jews from surrounding nations were in Jerusalem on the day of Pentecost. When the 120 people were baptized in the Holy Spirit and began speaking in other tongues, those Jews hearing them were amazed. They recognized that these Christians were speaking in the languages of the countries the Jews had traveled from. Then Peter preached a sermon so powerful that 3,000 people were converted that day. As these newly converted Christians returned to their homes, the gospel spread through the entire region. James wrote to the churches that had been established in the many nations surrounding his home city, Jerusalem.

Some have said, "James wrote to the Jews." But in James 1:2 he uses the words, "My brethren." So I believe that James had something bigger in mind. I believe that he was writing to all the children of his heavenly Father, all of the spiritual brothers to the Lord Jesus Christ. Therefore, James wrote to **you.**

Speaking Like Brothers

Sometimes we share God's Word with loved ones and get absolutely no response. Even worse, we get a hostile, negative response! We say, "They aren't getting it at all." But while appearances will lie, God's Word is true. Isaiah 55:11 promises you that God's Word never returns to Him void. Just as the Word changed James it pierces the hearts of unbelievers whether they like it or not!

James may not have believed in Jesus during His earthly ministry, yet the Word was still piercing his heart. When his spirit was awakened by the new birth, Jesus' teachings came to life within James, quickened to his remembrance by the Holy Spirit. This is beautifully confirmed in how the essence of James' message parallels the Lord's teaching (Matthew, chapters 5-7).

James:

"My brethren, count it all joy when ye fall into diverse temptations" (James 1:2).

Jesus:

"Blessed are they which are persecuted for righteousness' sake: for theirs is the kingdom of heaven. Blessed are ye when men shall revile you, and persecute you, and shall say all manner of evil against you falsely, for my sake. Rejoice, and be exceeding glad: for great is your reward in heaven: for so persecuted they the prophets which were before you" (Matthew 5:10-12).

Both Jesus and James said, "Rejoice in the face of adversity." As the Holy Spirit brought the words of Jesus to James' remembrance, I'm sure he also remembered the example his brother had presented during His earthly life. The words he once resented became words he taught others:

James:

"But let patience have her perfect work, that ye may be perfect and entire, wanting nothing" (James 1:4).

Jesus:

"Be ye therefore perfect, even as your Father which is in heaven is perfect" (Matthew 5:48).

First, Jesus said, "Be perfect." Ever practical, James said, "You will become perfect by exercising patience." In the book of James the word *perfect* means "mature." Patience yields maturity in every Christian.

We are an impatient generation. We have instant coffee, instant tea, and we want instant answers to prayer: "Lord, give me patience **now**!" God's Word, in contrast, teaches us to exercise patience. It is through patience that we reap the benefits of God's Word. James didn't believe in giving up. He believed in praying and waiting patiently for God's answer in every situation. An old story about James says that his knees were as tough as a camel's because he spent so much time praying on them! He learned his keys to maturity from the best teacher: Jesus.

James:

"If any of you lack wisdom, let him ask of God, that giveth to all men liberally, and upbraideth not; and it shall be given him" (James 1:5).

Jesus:

"Ask and it shall be given you; seek and ye shall find; knock, and it shall be opened unto you. If ye then, being evil, know how to give good gifts unto your children, how much more shall your Father which is in heaven give good things to them that ask him?" (Matthew 7:7,11).

First, Jesus said, "If you have a need, ask God to meet it." Then James made it practical: "If you have a need, get God's wisdom on how to handle your situation." You will obtain His wisdom **by asking for it.**

Compare Matthew 6:19-21 to an admonition by James:

James:

"Go to now, ye rich men, weep and howl for your miseries that shall come upon you. Your riches are corrupted, and your garments are moth-eaten. Your gold and silver is cankered; and the rust of them shall be a witness against you, and shall eat your flesh as it were fire. Ye have heaped treasure together for the last days" (James 5:1-3.)

Jesus:

"Lay not up for yourselves treasures upon earth, where moth and rust doth corrupt, and where thieves break through and steal; But lay up for yourselves treasures in heaven, where neither moth nor rust doth corrupt, and where thieves do not break through nor steal: For where your treasure is, there will your heart be also" (Matthew 6:19-21).

Sometimes we think, "If I had walked with Jesus during His earthly ministry I would have understood the scriptures." But James really blew it while Jesus was on the earth, and he saw the Lord nearly every day! On the other hand, the Apostle Paul had the most penetrating revelation of the Last Supper, and he was not even there. His perception of Christ's victory at the cross is outstanding, yet Paul never physically walked with the Lord.

All revelation knowledge of God's Word must come through the inspiration of the Holy Spirit. Jesus is called "the living Word." When He spoke God's Word, the Holy Spirit revealed its truth, and He still reveals it today! Isn't that encouraging? You don't have to wish that you had walked with the Lord. You can walk with Him today and every day as the Holy Spirit leads you into the truth of the scripture.

Walking With the Word

The word *walk* denotes activity! Don't ever assume that just because someone has been a Christian for a long time, he or she will be mature. That just isn't true! I know people who have been Christians for 35 years, and they are still spiritual children. Yet I know some new Christians who are very mature in the Lord. They attained maturity by acting on God's Word.

Do you want to be a mature Christian? The key to maturity found in the book of James is, "Practice God's Word in your life":

"But be ye doers of the word, and not hearers only, deceiving your own selves. For if any be a hearer of the word, and not a doer, he is like unto a man beholding his natural face in a glass: For he beholdeth himself, and goeth his way, and straightway forgetteth what manner of man he was. But whoso looketh into the perfect law of liberty, and continueth therein, he being not a forgetful hearer, but a doer of the work, this man shall be blessed in his deed" (James 1:22-25).

Jesus told a parable about two men who built houses: one house was built on sand, the other on a rock. The sand represented the hearing of God's Word without action; the rock represented the person who hears and obeys God's Word. You know the story: the wind and waves came against these houses, and only the house on the rock stood firmly intact. Both men heard the Word, but only one built a foundation by acting on it. The rock is a combination of hearing and doing.

The Holy Spirit reveals the scripture to us for one

reason: for us to act on it. God's will for us is equal to His Word. If we want to be mature Christians, our goal must be the same goal that Jesus had here on earth: to do the Father's will. That is how you will be a spiritual brother of the Lord:

"For whosoever shall do the will of my Father which is in heaven, the same is my brother, and sister, and mother" (Matthew 12:50).

Your Key to Victory

The first chapter of James is your key to victory in everything you do. The Bible says that Christians will experience various trials and temptations. It would be wonderful if we could say, "I'm a Christian so I will never have another trial." But while we cannot ignore the trials that come, God's Word says we can win over trials, and James tells us how:

"My brethren, count it all joy when ye fall into divers temptations" (James 1:2).

Does that scripture mean that in desperate situations you can still be happy? Yes! Once I asked God, "How can You expect me to have joy when everything looks so black? That seems impossible!" Then the Lord sweetly said, "The joy of the Lord is your strength."

Look at trials with a winning attitude. God wants you to win, and He has the strength to bring you through as a winner. Then you can be joyful, because victory is ahead. Your number-one strategy in trials should be to count them all joy.

James also tells you what to do while you're waiting for victory: "Knowing this, that the trying of your faith worketh patience" (James 1:3). Plan to be patient while you are counting it all joy. You will not find it hard to be patient when you know that it is God's will for you to win over trials and temptations.

You have to have faith **and** patience to inherit God's promises. Faith and patience are "Siamese twins"—one cannot be separated from the other. We can say, "I have world-overcoming faith!" But the faith will be tried. In order to have faith that endures, you must also have patience. Then the results are guaranteed:

> *"Let patience have her perfect work, that ye may be perfect and entire, wanting nothing" (James 1:4).*

As I have said, the word *perfect* really means "mature." The mature Christian understands that his faith wins over circumstances. When you can trust God patiently, your faith will make you win. Being patient is one of the Christian's most difficult tasks, but it also produces the greatest rewards!

Along with faith and patience, James gives you another element that is necessary for your victory:

> *"If any of you lack wisdom, let him ask of God, that giveth to all men liberally, and upbraideth not; and it shall be given him" (James 1:5).*

Did you ever look around at your circumstances and say, "Dear God, what am I going to do? This is the biggest mess I have ever seen!" That's the time to ask for God's wisdom. If you need wisdom, ask God for it and you will receive it. But you have to know how to ask for wisdom:

> *"But let him ask in faith, nothing wavering. For he that wavereth is like a wave of the sea driven with the wind and tossed. For let not that man think that he shall receive any thing of the Lord.*

A double minded man is unstable in all his ways"
(James 1:6-8).

After you ask God for wisdom to handle your trial, believe that God gave you that wisdom. If you ask for wisdom today, then tomorrow you are not to say, "I wonder whether I am hearing from God or not." You have to say, "God's Word promises that He gives me wisdom. Therefore, I believe that I have received His wisdom."

With all trials come temptations to worry, fear, and doubt God. Trials are external. They are on the outside, and have to do with our circumstances. But when trials come on the outside, then temptations come on the inside: "I don't know about being a Christian. God's Word doesn't seem to be helping my situation. Where is God in this?" Some people even blame God for having sent them trials. They say, "If God loved me, He would not do this to me."

James clearly said, *"Let no man say when he is tempted, that he is tempted of God"* (James 1:13). Satan is the one behind temptation. Hardships, trials, poverty, sickness and death are **all** from satan. Don't ever say, "God is doing this to me." He is not! God is not a child-abuser. Would you tempt your own children? Of course you wouldn't. Then you can be sure that God would certainly not tempt the children whom He loves. God wants to help you win, not lose.

The reason temptation comes is because we allow the devil to entice us with carnal thoughts. James 1:14 says, *"Every man is tempted, when he is drawn away of his own lust, and enticed."*

The two parts of your life the devil attacks are your

mind and emotions. What he really wants is your will. If he can convince your mind and emotions to listen to him, then with your will you choose to sin.

When satan came to Eve, he appealed to her emotions through lust. Satan made the fruit seem attractive to Eve, and she wanted to eat it. Then lust led to deception. Ultimately, lust affected the decision Eve made, and she gave her will over to the devil and sinned: *"Then when lust hath conceived, it bringeth forth sin, and sin, when it is finished, bringeth forth death."* In temptation, always remember that the devil is working on your mind and emotions to get you to sin, and bring death to yourself.

You say, "How can I keep from sinning?" James has given you three beautiful keys that tell you how to win over sin. The first one is, when you are tempted, look ahead at the result of sin: death.

Had Eve looked ahead, she would have said, "What has God said about eating this fruit?" Of course God had warned, "If you eat the fruit of the knowledge of good and evil, you will die." Eve could have looked ahead and seen death. When temptation comes your way, look ahead. Suddenly sin becomes far less attractive when you see that its price is death.

The second key to win over sin is found in James 1:17, *"Every good and every perfect gift is from above, and cometh down from the Father of lights, with whom is no variableness, neither shadow of turning."*

The devil told Eve, "God is holding out on you because you aren't as wise as He is. If you eat that fruit, you will be wise like Him." But that was a lie, wasn't it? Eve had all that she could have wanted. After all, she was created in God's own image. Eve could have avoided sin by looking around to all the blessings she had and seeing that every good and perfect gift is from above.

First look ahead, and then look around. Finally, there is one more place you can look; you can look within your heart to the power of God's Word: *"Of his own will begat he us with the word of truth, that we should be a kind of firstfruits of his creatures."*

Every born-again Christian has been begotten by God's Word. The Word within you will overcome the temptation around you. He that is in you is greater than he that is in the world.

God wants you to win over temptations and trials, and He gave you His Word to prove it. His Word will not only save you from temptation, it will keep you safe from it. But you have to stand fast on the Word. James 1:23 says, "For if any man be a hearer of the Word, and not a doer, he is like unto a man beholding his natural face in a glass." If I look into a mirror, I can see my face, but I cannot see my thoughts, my emotions, or my will. But if I look in the mirror of God's Word, I see God's supernatural power on my behalf:

"But whoso looketh into the perfect law of liberty and continueth therein, he being not a forgetful hearer, but a doer of the work, this man shall be blessed in his deed" (James 1:24).

In the mirror of God's Word, I can see whether my thoughts, my emotions, and my will line up with God's Word. I can tell my body, "Get in line with God's Word. The Bible says that Jesus bore my sickness on the cross." If my will is wavering, I tell it, "You are going to believe God's Word no matter how circumstances may appear."

Keep looking at God's Word. In His Word is the image of a winner, the image of a mature Christian. It is by looking at your overcoming image in God's Word that you endure and overcome temptation and trials. Watch what happens to those who win over temptation:

"Blessed is the man that endureth temptation. For when he is tried, he shall receive the crown of life, which the Lord hath promised to them that love him" (James 1:12).

The end of sin is death, but the end of your faith and patience is life. If you are in a trial, my advice to you is the same advice that James offered: "Count it all joy." You don't have a trial; you have an opportunity to receive a crown of life!

Chapter Two

DO THE WORD

When my husband and I first entered the full-time ministry in pastoring, my mother offered us some very wise advice: She said, "Never look to people as your source. Always look to God, and He will meet you—sometimes in surprising ways!" That's exactly what He has done.

Honey, Do It!

I remember teaching at an Episcopalian church during a time when we faced a financial crisis in our radio and television ministry. Not long after I had begun to teach at this church, an elderly couple walked in, sat down near the back of the room, and started to discuss something—loudly! They appeared to be arguing with each other. After I was finished teaching, the couple approached me to ask if I would have lunch with them. The Lord prompted me, "Go."

When we sat down in the restaurant the woman asked me, "How much does it cost to buy radio time?" She seemed interested in being on the radio personally. I answered, "It costs $15.50 a day in Denver." (It cost much less then!)

"No," she pressed, "that isn't what I meant. I want to know what you pay for one year of broadcasting." I multiplied the amount and told her what it was. Then she turned to her husband and said, "Honey, write Marilyn a check for $6,000." I thought, "Honey, do it!"

That woman had traveled from another city to attend the Bible study because the Lord had instructed her to pay for a year of my radio broadcasting. She had no earthly idea that the ministry was confronting a serious financial need. She was simply obeying God.

"Did she look wealthy?" No! From appearances you would have thought I should have written **her** a check. But God is our source and He knows our needs.

According to James, the first step of walking by faith is to get our eyes off people and on God:

"My brethren, do not hold your faith in our glorious Lord Jesus with an attitude of respect of persons. For if there come into your assembly a man with a gold ring in goodly apparel, and there come in also a poor man in vile raiment; And ye have respect unto him that weareth the gay clothing, and say unto him, Sit thou there in a good place; and say to the poor, Stand thou there, or sit under my footstool: Are ye not then partial in yourselves and are become judges of evil thoughts?" (James 2:1-4, NAS-KJV).

To prefer one person above another is to enter into judgment. God does not want us to judge others by their material status. James calls this attitude "respect of persons;" I call it "pyramid-climbing." But even in James' correction there is love. James calls us "my brethren."

He never uses God's Word to hurt people; he shows us what is wrong and then reveals a better way to handle our situations.

Why would someone be a respecter of persons? No one can pull his coat around himself and say, "I've never done that!" We have all been guilty of pyramid-climbing, sometimes without even realizing it. Then later the Lord convicts us about it and we pray, "God, how could that have happened?" What is respect of persons? Basically, it takes place when a person desires personal gain for himself, and he is looking to people to put him over, instead of looking to God.

If we will stop looking for personal gain from other people and put our trust in God, then we open the door for Him to bless us with every blessing of His kingdom:

"Hearken, my beloved brethren, Hath not God chosen the poor of this world rich in faith, and heirs of the kindgom which he hath promised to them that love him?" (James 2:5).

When we look to God in faith, we find that as heirs to God's kingdom, everything that God has is ours. Why look for rich men to meet our needs? God is far richer than any man: He's got it all!

If the kingdom of God has every treasure we could desire for this life and the next life, we must look to God as our source in every situation. This is the first key of not being a respecter of persons. When we look to God, people's appearances no longer matter. We'll be equally kind to every person: we'll be walking in the spirit of love.

Jesus had an outstanding reputation for not being a respecter of persons. Jesus was James' example, so let's make Him our example:

"And they sent out unto him their disciples with the Herodians, saying, Master, we know that thou art true, and teachest the way of God in truth, neither carest thou for any man: for thou **regardest not the person of men"** *(Matthew 22:16).*

Jesus treated every person alike. Rich, poor, young, old, the Lord loved them all. He had the wonderful ability to look past a person's physical appearance and see his potential.

The Lord was equally loving at a well when He talked with a despised Samaritan woman. The religious people of Jesus' day disdained the Samaritans and did everything possible to avoid them. But Jesus went out of His way, not only to talk to a Samaritan, but to a Samaritan woman at that! In His disciples' eyes, the woman was a second-class citizen. In the Lord's eyes she was beloved of God. The words Jesus spoke so stirred her spirit that she was converted and became an evangelist! She turned her whole city around because, by faith, Jesus looked at her potential.

Consider Matthew, a disciple who was a hated tax collector before he received the Lord's call to discipleship. By Jewish standards, Matthew was a turn-coat because he collected taxes for the Romans. As far as the Jews were concerned, anyone on the Roman payroll was an enemy. At that time, Rome had no stable tax system, so the tax collectors padded the required tax and used the extra money to feather their own nest. When Jesus called to Matthew, "Follow Me," we probably would have said, "Not him, Lord!" But Matthew

Do The Word

was one of the Lord's most faithful, loyal men. His touching gospel portrays Jesus as "The King."

First, we are to see God as our source; second, we are to look past people's appearances to see their possibilities in the Lord. I'm not saying, "Ignore what you see; pretend it isn't there at all." We must allow the Lord to give us His vision for others. So often we want to judge people by their past or present, but God says, "Accept them where they are. Then develop a faith vision for their futures."

Barnabas had a marvelous ministry in receiving a faith vision for the ministries of others and then helping them to develop their ministries. While the Apostle Paul was still called "Saul," Barnabas was instrumental in gaining credence for him with the other disciples. The disciples heard that Saul had been converted, but they were unwilling to believe it. They said, "His conversion is a farce! He's killing Christians." But with Barnabas' intervention, the disciples recognized the truth of Saul's ministry. Soon afterward his name became "Paul."

Barnabas and Paul ventured out together on the first missionary journey. On it, Barnabas met a young man whose ministry he was to develop. That young man was named John Mark. Shortly after Paul, Barnabas and John Mark departed, the latter developed a terrible case of homesickness and had to return to his city. Later he wanted to accompany Paul and Barnabas on the second missionary journey, but Paul sharply refused to offer him a second chance. A major disagreement ensued between Paul and Barnabas who said, "If John Mark doesn't go, I won't go either."

What a people-oriented person Barnabas was! He was

so insistent in pleading John Mark's case. Paul and Silas departed in one direction, and that day Barnabas' development of young John Mark's ministry began. The teaching John Mark received was so effective that later Paul wrote a letter saying, "Please send me John Mark. He is profitable in the ministry."

How could Barnabas have known that Saul would become Paul? How did he perceive that John Mark would mature and write the gospel of Mark by the inspiration of the Holy Spirit? John 7:24 gives you a key to Barnabas' fine discernment:

"Judge not according to the appearance, but judge righteous judgment" (John 7:24).

As Christians we will only see God's vision for others if we are walking in love toward them. Faith must be motivated by love. If we don't love every person with Christ's love, we fail to walk by faith. But when we commit to loving them as He did, then we see beyond a person's appearance to his potential.

I'll never forget Susie. Her life is a perfect example of why we must not permit appearances to discourage our faith for someone's future. In our church's early years, Susie was a member of the youth group I taught. She specialized in creating disturbances. At times I sat behind Susie to maintain some order during the church services. If I had to correct her she would glare at me as if to say, "I hate you!"

One day Susie hitchhiked to another state. Whenever my husband saw her mother he would ask, "How is Susie? If you hear from her, tell her I love her." For years we did not hear a word from her, but according to her mother she was always in some type of trouble.

When she was 21 years old, Susie came back to town. One evening she came to our church and sat near the back. We had no idea that she was present. That night as my husband preached, the Lord convicted Susie, "I'm not going to deal with you any longer."

That night Susie came to the altar and gave her heart unreservedly to the Lord. She became strongly involved in our youth group, and has since then attended Bible college, married, and entered the full-time ministry.

Never judge a person by his or her inadequacies. If you do, you'll be discouraged. James says that if we don't show the Lord's love to people, we are in sin:

"If ye fulfill the royal law according to the scripture, Thou shalt love thy neighbor as thyself, ye do well: But if ye have respect to persons, ye commit sin, and are convinced of the law as transgressors. For whosoever shall keep the whole law, and yet offend in one point, he is guilty of all" (James 2:8-10).

James placed such a wholehearted emphasis on God's Word. In chapter one he spoke of *"the word of truth"* (1:18), *"the engrafted word"* (1:21), and *"the perfect law of liberty"* (1:25). In chapter two James spoke of *"the royal law"* (2:8), *"the scripture"* (2:8,23), *"the law"* (2:9,10), and again, *"the law of liberty"* (2:12).

James did not reason with those whom he taught, nor did he state his opinions. He built a solid foundation of correction on God's Word. Then he pointed in the right direction. He didn't just say, "Don't be a respecter of persons!" He said, "Fulfill the royal law: love everyone."

I once asked the Lord, "Why is love the royal law?"

He answered, "Because it will cause you to live like a king." We are kings and priests in Christ Jesus. We have been ordained to live by a law of supernatural love. Love is to rule our hearts, and consequently our actions:

"So speak ye, and so do, as they that shall be judged by the law of liberty" (James 2:12).

Something very special happens when we esteem the royal law of love: it becomes a law of liberty to us. The more you read, speak, and act on God's Word, the more it becomes an integral part of your soulish nature. We don't always feel like acting on God's Word. We don't always feel like reading our Bibles. But we obey God and do those things because we love Him. At first God's Word is as a law to us. But the more we make that law a part of our lives, the freer we become. The day will arrive when we react spontaneously according to God's Word! God's Word becomes a law of liberty: it sets us free to act in His love.

Faith With Works: A Product of Love

People think that the second chapter of James is primarily about faith that produces works. But before James could address the subject of faith, he had to lay a foundation for love. Love is a fruit of the spirit; it is a resident within every Christian by the power of the Holy Spirit. Love is not a "feeling." It is a decision. We decide to act in the love of God toward people.

I think that most Christians get into trouble by trying to live out their own love (feelings), instead of living out God's love (a decision to put others first). Love is activated by our wills.

James corrected those people who were respecters of persons by saying, "Walk by love, the royal law." Then he progressed to what love should produce: faith and works.

In James 2:14-19, three kinds of faith are revealed: intellectual faith, emotional faith, and dynamic faith:

> *"What doth it profit, my brethren, though a man say he hath faith, and have not works? can faith save him? If a brother or sister be naked, and destitute of daily food, And one of you say unto them, Depart in peace, be ye warmed and filled; notwithstanding ye give them not those things which are needful to the body; what doth it profit? Even so faith, if it hath not works, is dead, being alone. Yea, a man may say, "Thou hast faith, and I have works: shew me thy faith without thy works, and I will shew thee my faith by my works. Thou believest that there is one God; thou doest well: the devils also believe and tremble" (James 2:14-19).*

True faith that works by love will produce works in the life of every Christian. James says, "Any faith that does not produce works is dead."

First James showed a man whose faith was solely in his mind. That man never moved past intellectual acknowledgement of God's Word. If he truly believed in God's Word, he would feed the person who was destitute of food. But the man without faith was hindered by his mind. Perhaps he thought, "Why doesn't this person get a job?" This type of intellectual reasoning blocks true dynamic faith.

James said, "Even the devils do more than give intellectual assent to God's Word. They tremble." That's emotional, honey! The demons believe, so they have intellectual faith. They tremble, so faith is also in their emotions. But emotional faith is not saving faith, is it? This faith substitutes **words** for **works,** and without works, it is dead.

I looked up the word *dead* and found that it means "barren." A more colorful description would mean "it draws no interest." If you put your money in a savings account, you would expect your money to produce some added gain for you. If it gained interest, your money would be considered productive and profitable. In the same way, faith should produce works in order to be productive and profitable to you.

Intellectual or emotional faith is not profitable to anyone. The devils cannot be saved, but they believe more than some people do. For one thing, they believe in eternal punishment:

> *"And they besought him that he would not command them to go out into the deep" (Luke 8:31).*

Devils also believe that Jesus is the Son of God:

> *"And the unclean spirits, when they saw him, fell down before him, and cried, saying, Thou art the Son of God" (Mark 3:11).*

I was raised in a church that did not believe in eternal punishment. The general belief was, "The only hell you have is here." Demons are smarter than that!

You say, "How can I have faith that supersedes my intellect and emotions?" You have faith that produces works by deciding to be a doer of God's Word and not a hearer only. Just as you decided to believe God when you received salvation, you can believe Him and act on His Word every day of your life. You want to please God? Live by faith in His Word.

Your mind may not always want to act in faith; you may not want to act in faith; but your *will* determines true faith: "God's Word is true, so I will act on it."

Abraham, "the father of faith," is a brilliant example of faith in action. Notice how James gives you examples of people from God's Word:

"Was not Abraham our father justified by works, when he had offered Isaac his son upon the altar? Seest thou how faith wrought with his works, and by works was faith made perfect? And the scripture was fulfilled which saith, Abraham believed God, and it was imputed unto him for righteousness: and he was called the Friend of God" (James 2:21-23).

God gave Abraham and his wife Sarah a child of promise named Isaac. Before that, they had been barren of children. Isaac was born from their faith in the miracle power of God's Word: "He said we would have a child, so we will have a child." One day, God told Abraham, I want you to offer your son, Isaac, as a sacrifice to Me on the mountain range of Moriah."

How could Abraham endure the intellectual and emotional pain of parting with his only son, his child of promise? The answer is in Hebrews 11:17-19:

"By faith Abraham, when he was tried, offered up Isaac: and he that had received the promises offered up his only begotten son, Of whom it was said, That in Isaac shall thy seed be called: Accounting that God was able to raise him up, even from the dead; from whence also he received him in a figure" (Hebrews 11:17-19).

Abraham made a decision to believe God's Word. He

37

said, "God promised me a child. Even if He has to raise Isaac from the ashes, He will give me a child." When Abraham made a decision in his heart to believe God, his emotions and intellect were transformed.

Emotionally, Abraham had the strength to lift the knife that would kill his own child. That's a heavy thought when you understand the bond of love between parent and child. Intellectually, Abraham's thoughts were affected: "I see my child raised from the dead." Physically, Abraham carried out God's Word.

As Abraham lifted the knife to kill Isaac, an angel spoke to him, "Life up your eyes." Looking up, Abraham saw a ram tangled in a nearby thicket. That ram would be Isaac's substitution in the sacrifice. Through this substitution Abraham received a revelation of the perfect sacrifice: There on the mountain range of Moriah, Abraham saw that the only Son of God would become the substitution for sinful man. He would be crucified on Calvary, in that same range of mountains. Abraham said, "On this mount it shall be seen."

Abraham was the first man to see resurrection! He believed in resurrection before it had happened. But he could not have seen it if his faith had not produced works. He saw the Lord's sacrifice of love for mankind—God's faith produced works, too! Then Abraham said, "I have met Jehovah Jireh."

The word *jireh* comes from a Hebrew verb meaning "to see." By calling God "Jehovah Jireh," Abraham was saying, "The Lord sees ahead to my needs, and then makes provision to meet them. He prepared a ram for the sacrifice even before I came to Moriah." Further, Abraham was saying, "God sees and prepares for everything I will ever do, and all I will ever be." That's really getting your faith in gear!

God has already made provision for every situation you will ever encounter. That alone should inspire your faith. In this life we will always be faced by situations we didn't plan for. But God saw those situations ahead, so we can look to Him and know that He has made provision for us in those times.

My natural instinct is to make plans. I plan activities weeks, months, even years in advance. Sometimes God allows me to plan this way; other times He doesn't. But when "plans" fall through, I know that He is Jehovah Jireh, and He will still put me over. The following story explains what I mean.

Once I was scheduled to teach in Las Vegas, but my flight was seriously delayed. Hours began to creep by, and I began to wonder if I would be on time to teach. Then the plane's captain told the passengers, "Go to lunch. When you return we will have a report on the scheduling."

That was not very encouraging! We still had no guarantee that the plane would leave soon. In situations like this, long-range planning is not an alternative. There were two options: I could lose my peace over the situation, or I could look to God as Jehovah Jireh. I said, "God, You opened the door for me to go to that city, so You'll have to help me walk through it."

I hunted for another ticket counter, praying quietly in the Spirit as I walked along. One counter advertised a flight departing for Las Vegas at 12:30. "But," the agent insisted, "this flight is booked. There are so many stand-bys that it's doubtful you could take this flight."

What happened? I was the last stand-by that was accepted! God had already seen the difficulty that I would encounter, and He had made a provision for it. Jehovah Jireh always sees ahead to take care of needs such as these.

Knowing God as Jehovah Jireh should change the way you react to crises. Fussing and fuming won't change circumstances, but Jehovah Jireh will!

God saw ahead and made the provision for a woman named Rahab. He saw her faith, and when Joshua sent two spies into the Promised Land, they "happened" to end up at Rahab's door:

"Likewise also was not Rahab the harlot justified by works, when she had received the messengers, and had sent them out another way?" (James 2:25).

I like the contrast James has given us. First he tells us about Abraham, a Jew and "the father of faith." Then he tells us about Rahab, who was not only a Gentile, but also a harlot. Looking at the examples, you might think they are incompatible. But the compatibility between Abraham and Rahab was not their outward appearances—it was their faith.

Rahab was so special. She heard the same rumor that was heard by all the people in Canaan (the Promised Land): The God of Israel opened the Red Sea; He killed their enemies Sihon and Og. Rahab, along with the rest of the Canaanites, knew that the Israelites would conquer their city, Jericho. Every person had heard the same report. What was different about Rahab? The difference was that Rahab **believed,** and her faith brought activity.

When the Hebrew spies sneaked into Canaan, Rahab was so excited that they had come to her home. She wanted the men to tell her about their wonderful God! She told them, "I have heard about your God." She had **heard!** How does faith come? Faith comes by hearing God's Word. Rahab heard the Word of God, believed it, and then confessed her faith out of her mouth. Romans 10:9 says, *"If thou shalt confess with thy mouth the Lord Jesus, and shalt believe in thine heart that God hath raised him from the dead, thou shalt be saved."* Faith always begins with hearing, believing and then confessing.

Rahab told the spies, "Your God is the God of the heavens and the earth." Intellectually and emotionally, Rahab believed. Then her faith brought action.

You can be sure that when you determine to act in faith, you will be tested. Rahab's test put not only her faith, but also her life on the line:

> *"And it was told the king of Jericho, saying, Behold, there came men in hither to night of the children of Israel to search out the country. And the king of Jericho sent unto Rahab, saying, Bring forth the men that are come to thee, which are entered into thine house: for they be come to search out all the country" (Joshua 2:2,3).*

Rahab's countrymen came to her door and said, "Bring us the Hebrew spies. We know they are in your house." But she so strongly believed in the goodness of their God, she had hidden the Hebrew spies from sight. Rahab's faith was so great that she risked her life for the defense of God's people. She said, "The spies were here, but they have already gone.''

It's one thing to say, "I believe." It's another thing to act on what you believe. True faith always brings activity. Rahab esteemed the God of Israel above her own countrymen. She was such a smart woman, too. After the men had left, she asked the spies, "How can I be sure I'll be saved?" The spies told her, "Hang a cord out your window. When we take the city, you will be spared."

Rahab had such wonderful faith, she even believed for the salvation of her whole family:

'And that ye will save alive my father, and my mother, and my brethren, and my sisters, and all that they have, and deliver our lives from death''
(Joshua 2:13).

What is the first thing most new converts do? They hand you a prayer list with the names of all their unsaved loved ones. Rahab did the same thing. She wanted her whole family to know the Lord. This is not just intellectual or emotional faith—this is dynamic! We will see the results of her marvelous faith.

The Israelites never even had to fight a battle to conquer Jericho. God had a different plan. He said, "For six days in a row, march around the city one time. On the seventh day, march around the city seven times. When you are through marching, the priests will blow their trumpets, all the people will shout, and the walls of Jericho will fall down. The city will be yours."

On the seventh day the Israelites marched around Jericho seven times. Then the priests blew their trumpets, the people all shouted, and as God had promised, Jericho's walls came crumbling to the ground.

Only one wall was left standing; Rahab's wall remained erect, a tribute to her saving faith.

Can you have faith that your life will stand while around you everyone else's walls are crumbling? We live in a sinful day: families are breaking up, children are going astray. But we can follow Rahab's example by believing God's Word and acting upon it.

Total Surrender

James has said, "True faith has works." Having emotional and intellectual faith is not enough. Our will must be involved, causing us to match faith with works. But does God want us to be emotionally and intellectually involved in faith also? Yes! He wants faith to be a part of our whole being. The more of ourselves that we surrender to God, the greater our faith will be.

The book of Jonah shows us how God wants faith to be demonstrated in every area of our lives. Our minds, our bodies, our emotions and our words are all to be full of faith. If not, God will deal with us to get in line with His Word. He had to deal with Jonah.

The book of Jonah begins with God telling him, "Go command the people of Nineveh to repent."

Jonah's answer was an unqualified, "NO!" Nineveh was the capital of the Assyrian nation, and the Assyrians were some of the most vicious, brutal people of their day. They had been murdering Jonah's people, and he certainly did not want them to repent. He wanted God to destroy them.

As Jonah saw it, the logical way for God to deal with Nineveh was to pour His wrath out on them in destruction. Emotionally, he hated the people of Nineveh. I'm sure Jonah also feared the people, and thought, "If I preach to them, they will kill me." With all of this inner turmoil, Jonah refused to obey God. Instead, he fled in the opposite direction of Nineveh in a boat with some other men.

As Jonah and the men sailed away, a cruel storm arose and death for all seemed certain. When the men found out that Jonah was fleeing from the call of God, they recognized the storm to be God's judgment. Jonah was cast into the sea, and he ended up in the belly of a great fish. There, he finally submitted his will to the Lord:

> *"When my soul fainted within me I remembered the Lord: and my prayer came in unto thee in thine holy temple. They that observe lying vanities forsake their own mercy. But I will sacrifice unto thee with the voice of thanksgiving; I will pay that I have vowed. Salvation is of the Lord" (Jonah 2:7-9).*

When Jonah submitted his will to God, God caused the fish to vomit Jonah out on the shore. From there, he went immediately to Nineveh and commanded the people, "Repent!"

Jonah's simple message sparked a tremendous revival. The people of Nineveh fasted, and they were so sincere that even their animals were put on a fast! God turned the whole picture around, and it really shocked Jonah. He certainly did not expect the people of Nineveh to receive his message; in fact, he was hoping they wouldn't receive it. When God corrected the spiritual condition of the people of Nineveh, Jonah fell apart, started to cry, and even said, "I wish I could die."

You see, Jonah had enough faith to obey God, but not enough faith to handle the results of his obedience. Because of Jonah's self-pity, God withered a vine that had been giving Jonah shade. Then God said, "You had pity on a gourd that withered before your eyes, but you don't care about those thousands of people in Nineveh. What's your problem?"

Jonah's problem was his attitude. He obeyed God, but his attitude was rotten: "There! You told me to, so I did it!" God had to reprimand him, "Faith should involve your entire being. I want your spirit, your mind, your emotions, and your actions all surrendered to Me."

Did Jonah ever get it right? I believe he did, because he authored the book of Jonah. He would not have "told on himself" if his attitude had remained poor. He lined his attitude up with God's Word.

How did Jonah end up caring for—even loving—his enemies? He brought his emotions into faith by an act of his will. He said, "If God loves them, I love them, too."

Faith is just that simple. It is the surrender of your will to God's love. God deals with unsurrendered areas of our life because He wants us to be 100% in faith. When your whole being is in faith, you'll be a doer of God's Word. That is dynamic faith.

Chapter Three

PART I
YIELD YOUR TONGUE
TO GOD'S WORD

Most people want to be chiefs, not Indians. They want spiritual maturity to happen to them overnight. James, in his potent chapter on the tongue, seems to say, "You'll never be a good chief until you've been a good Indian." For all Christians, controlling the tongue is essential to being either a good leader or follower.

The commitment a church leader makes to God must be airtight, or the pressure of leadership will break him. Church leaders are subject to much criticism because they deal with so many people. James opened his third chapter by revealing that, while Christian leadership looks attractive, it is difficult:

"My brethren, be not many masters, knowing that we shall receive the greater condemnation" (James 3:1).

James was saying, "Do you really want to be a leader? Then you are accountable to God for many other souls, in addition to yourself." For even the most mature Christians, leadership has its drawbacks:

"For in many things we offend all" (James 3:2a).

I'd love to be able to say, "I've never offended anyone." But as a pastor's wife over a large congregation, offenses have come. James knew the key to eliminating offenses and accelerating Christian maturity. The key is in the control of our tongues.

"If any man offend not in word, the same is a perfect man, and able also to bridle the whole body" (James 3:2b).

The word *perfect* in the above passage means "mature." Therefore, James is telling us that a man's mark of maturity is found in his speech. If you desire spiritual growth, examine the words that you speak. Through controlling your words, you control your thoughts, emotions, and physical body. The choice is yours: your tongue can destroy; it can direct; and it can delight.

Your Tongue Can Destroy

During the war, my father worked in a shipyard in Pennsylvania. On the walls throughout the old shipyard were huge posters cautioning workers, "Loose lips can sink ships." The workers were required to be secretive about their work. Too much said could have cost our countrymen's lives.

Our loose lips can sink our ships if we don't guard our words. Generations of children have boasted, "Sticks and stones can break my bones, but words can never harm me." Words can harm and even destroy us, and the people around us. Whether spoken for good or for evil, words keep working long after they have been spoken.

Yet, as hard as we try, it seems impossible to bridle our own speech. Have you ever tried? After saying something really negative, you vow, "I'll never say that again." But two weeks later, you're saying things that are even worse! James said that no man can control his tongue:

"For every kind of beasts, and of birds, and of serpents, and of things in the sea, is tamed, and hath been tamed of mankind: But the tongue can no man tame; it is an unruly evil, full of deadly poison" (James 3:7,8).

Negative words are like poison. Speaking negative words turns your tongue into an agent of destruction. Those words can defile your whole body and cause as much damage as a bite inflicted by a poisonous animal.

Who is behind poisonous words? Hell itself is behind them. Our wrong words may begin as a small fire, but even the smallest of fires is capable of setting a whole forest ablaze. Proverbs 26 says that the source of fiery words is strife:

"Where no wood is, there the fire goeth out; so where there is no talebearer, the strife ceaseth. As coals are to burning coals, and wood to fire;

so is a contentious man to kindle strife'' (Proverbs 26:20,21).

God hates the spreading of strife among men who are supposed to be brothers! If you are stirring up hatred among people, you are just hurting yourself. Do yourself a favor: stop setting fires and start putting them out with God's Word.

You say, "I don't speak negative words." Do you listen to others speaking them? If you listen, you are as guilty as the person speaking. If someone wants to tell you a story about another individual, confront the talebearer. Ask him, "Have you discussed this with the other person?"

Usually the person's answer will be, "No, I haven't." Then you can settle the matter using God's Word. Matthew 18:15 says that Christians are to confront specifically the offending person in a spirit of love to correct him. If Christians will solve disagreements with scripture, there will be far less strife among brothers. Just as Christ made peace between man and God, our goal should be to maintain peace among ourselves. 1 Corinthians 13:6 says, *"Love does not rejoice in unrighteousness, but rejoices with the truth."* Love your spiritual brothers enough not to spread bad news about them.

God doesn't even want us associating with speakers of evil (Proverbs 11:13). Why? Because sin is contagious. We become like those with whom we spend time. I have found that the people who talk the most are usually the ones who cause the most trouble:

"He that hath knowledge spareth his words: and a man of understanding is of an excellent spirit" (Proverbs 17:27).

I looked up the word *excellent,* and it means "cool." A man with understanding will keep his cool. On the other hand, a hot heart leads to burning words. If you don't want to be a hothead, watch what you say. A perfect man will control his words, thereby controlling his entire life.

Your Tongue Can Direct

The bit and the rudder both signify direction. You will either direct yourself into life, or into death:

"Death and life are in the power of the tongue: and they that love it shall eat the fruit thereof" (Proverbs 18:21).

There is only one way to guarantee that you will speak words of life. To speak words filled with life, you must first put those words in your heart:

"For out of the abundance of the heart the mouth speaketh. A good man out of the good treasure of the heart bringeth forth good things: and an evil man out of the evil treasure of the heart bringeth forth evil things" (Matthew 12:34b, 35).

Your heart is like a vault where you store the treasure of God's Word. If you want to withdraw life-filled words, you must first deposit the treasure. When you do, you will be prepared to speak words that will direct you in God's perfect will.

Once I was invited to speak at a luncheon for congressional wives in Washington, D.C. Shortly after the committee in Washington had scheduled me to speak, they called back and said, "The luncheon has been cancelled." I immediately began to speak God's Word over the situation: "I trust in the Lord with all my heart and lean not unto my own understanding. I acknowledge Him in all my ways, and He directs my paths."

I told my staff, "The luncheon may have been postponed, but it has not been cancelled." Only three days after the cancellation, a committee member called to tell my secretary, "We are scheduling the luncheon one day earlier. Can Marilyn be there?"

Just as God's Word kept a door open for His perfect will in my life, His Word will keep doors open for you. **Practice** God's Word, don't just read it. Your tongue will direct you in God's will if, through practice, you build an immovable foundation for victory.

Your Tongue Can Delight

The fountain and the fig tree are both sources of delight and refreshing. James wasn't the only one who likened your tongue to a tree; so did King Solomon:

"The law of the wise is as a fountain of life, to depart from the snares of death" (Proverbs 13:14).

"The words of a man's mouth are as deep waters, and the wellspring of wisdom as a flowing brook" (Proverbs 18:4).

God's Word refreshes you in any situation, and as you speak the Word, you bring refreshing to others. In the Old Testament, the priest washed his hands and feet in a brazen laver before he entered the holy place. The laver was made from mirrors, so the priest could see himself as he washed. After having walked through the hot desert sand and handled the bloody sacrifices for sin, the priest found cleansing and refreshing in the cool water. Likewise, the mirror of God's Word reminds us of who we are in Christ, and brings us cleansing and refreshing:

"That he might sanctify and cleanse it (the church) with the washing of the water by the word, That he might present it to himself a glorious church, not having spot, or wrinkle, or any such thing; but that it should be holy and without blemish" (Ephesians 5:26,27).

Speaking God's Word gives you continuous cleansing power that works on the inside and reveals itself on the outside. Only when your heart is full of the Word can it produce God's cleansing and refreshing. Then, as you speak that Word, you become spiritually equipped to be a priest to others.

The Word in your mouth proves to others that you belong to God, and that you are the righteousness of God in Christ:

"The mouth of a righteous man is a well of life" (Proverbs 10:11a).

As a righteous one, God's Word in your mouth brings life to others. James compared your tongue to a tree, which brings life through fruitbearing. A tree that is barren of fruit fails to benefit anyone. But by speaking God's Word, your vocabulary becomes fruitful. Jesus said, *"These words that I speak unto you, they are Spirit, and they are* life" (John 6:63).

We would never think of killing another person. But unfruitful speech such as gossip or lying brings death. Proverbs 12:22 says, *"Lying lips are an abomination to the Lord: but they that deal truly are his delight."* Purpose to bring life by dealing truly with others: bring them the truth of God's Word. Then you delight yourself, you delight others, and—best of all, you delight God. He is pleased when you bring weary souls His Word of refreshing:

"The Lord God hath given me the tongue of the learned, that I should know how to speak a word in season to him that is weary: he wakeneth me 10rning by morning, he wakeneth mine ear to 1ear as the learned" (Isaiah 50:4).

Are your words a tree of life? Make it your daily prayer that God will give you the tongue of the learned. Purpose to fill your heart with God's Word, and you will always have the right word to speak in the right season.

Remember, you will never bring life through your own inspiration. I have heard people say, "Some people are just Pollyanna's." But being Pollyanna's won't cut it with God. Only God's Word will not return void. Only as we saturate ourself with God's Word will we have the inspiration to speak as the learned. We must first hear God's voice in His Word, if we desire to become His voice to others.

One of the mothers in our church congregation was that voice to her daughter. She had raised her daughter in an environment where drinking alcoholic drinks was unacceptable. But one day the girl told her mother, "I drank wine at a friend's house last night, and I enjoyed it." The girl's mother called me on the telephone and asked me, "What should I tell my daughter? We enjoy an open, close relationship that I don't want to damage. Yet, I do not want her to acquire a taste for wine."

The girl's mother and I prayed in the Spirit, and then

went to the scripture for our answer. The Old Testament says that wine *"bites like a snake"* (Proverbs 23:32). The New Testament says *"Don't be drunk with wine, but be filled with the Spirit"* (Ephesians 5:18).

That afternoon the woman sat down with her daughter and counseled her by the wisdom of God's Word. She said, "Honey, wine gives you a pleasant feeling, but it's a counterfeit for the real thing." As they shared the scriptures, the daughter hugged her mother and said, "I see that. Don't worry about me, Mother."

That woman could have rebuked her daughter, and her rebuke would have destroyed the quality of communication they shared. She could have said, "You let me down. I'm disappointed in you." But she didn't say that. Instead, she gave her daughter God's Word, knowing that God's Word does not return void. God's Word brings life, not death; it brings conviction, not condemnation. When you fill your heart with God's Word, you become a bearer of His life.

You have been transformed by God's Word. Now He is calling you to be a transformer by sharing His Word with others. Place your hand over your mouth and dedicate your speech to the Lord:

"Dear Heavenly Father, I give you my tongue. I don't want to defile; I want to refresh and cleanse. I want to build others in the name of Jesus. Father, I repent of having spoken any corrupt communication. I dedicate my tongue to be used for your glory. In Jesus' name. Amen."

Now put your hand on your heart, because you must speak from the abundance of God's Word within your heart:

"Dear Father, I know that my heart was created for the abundance of Your Word. Today I give You my heart. I commit myself to seeking You daily in Your Word. Out of that abundance I will speak life to myself and to others. In Jesus' name. Amen."

James said, "You cannot tame your tongue." But God can tame your tongue! There was a beautiful taming of the tongue that came on the day of Pentecost. James was in the Upper Room with 120 other people when flames of fire appeared above them, and they began to speak in other tongues. That's a good fire, isn't it? This is the kind of fire we should be setting every day!

I cannot emphasize strongly enough the importance of praying in tongues. Paul said, "I speak in tongues more than you all," in his letter to the Corinthians. Where did Paul receive the inspiration to write one-third of the New Testament? I believe much of that inspiration came through speaking in tongues: Paul's tongue belonged to God.

If you want the fire of God's power in your life, begin praying in the Spirit as often as possible. As you yield your tongue to God, His fire burns the chaff from your life. The mark of maturity is found in the one whose tongue is dedicated to God.

Chapter Three

PART II

SPEAK WORDS THAT
MOVE MOUNTAINS

What do a horse's bit, ship's rudder, fire, poisonous animal, fountain, and fig tree have in common? James compared each of these to the tongue in his powerful study on the importance of the words we speak.

James wanted us to know that we can direct our lives into good or evil with our tongues. If we say, "The Lord is the strength of my life," our words create strength in our bodies. But if we say, "I'm getting old and forgetful," our words create weakness. Your tongue will either defile or sanctify you.

James said, *"Behold, we put bits in the horses' mouths, that they may obey us; and we turn about their whole body."* If you've ever been around horses, you know that they get some wild ideas. A horse's mind may say, "I don't want to go that way." His body may say, "I won't follow you." But a bit in the mouth of a horse overcomes his mind and emotions, and directs his actions. By comparing the horse's bit to a tongue, James was saying, "Your words control your mind, your emotions, and your physical body."

Your tongue can also overwhelm external circumstances. A ship comes across contrary forces of wind and waves during storms, yet a small device on the ship, called a "rudder," can guide the ship into a safe harbor. When life's storms come, our words decide whether we shipwreck or survive.

I call the tongue, "The world's smallest but largest troublemaker." James was more blunt: *"The tongue is a fire, a world of iniquity: so is the tongue among our members, that it defileth the whole body, and setteth on fire the course of nature; and it is set on fire of hell"* (James 3:6).

If I speak vicious words against a person, those words are backed by the power of hell. When a cruel statement reaches the person about whom it was spoken, it has become a blazing fire. One wrongly-spoken phrase can cause terrible damage.

We do so many things to improve our quality of life. Some of us lift weights; others observe careful diets. Yet because our tongues are the greatest factor of control in our lives, our greatest concern should be to bridle our tongues. King David knew the importance of controlling his speech. He prayed, "God, set a watch over my mouth." The Apostle Paul said, "Don't speak any corrupt communication."

Your Best Asset

On the positive side, you can speak heaven on earth. Proverbs 15:4 says, *" A wholesome tongue is a tree of life.''* Your tongue can be your worst liability or your finest asset. If it is to be an asset, you speak those words which please the Lord:

> *"Wherefore, holy brethren, partakers of the heavenly calling, consider the Apostle and High Priest of our profession, Christ Jesus" (Hebrews 3:1).*

The word *profession* is the Greek word *homoglia,* and it means "speaking the same thing." Do you want to speak the same words as Jesus? Then speak God's Word.

When you speak the Word, Jesus tells the Father what you have spoken. Jesus is the "High Priest," or "Mediator" of your confession. God is pleased when you speak His Word, because then He can bring it to pass in your life:

> *"I create the fruit of the lips; Peace, peace to him that is far off, and to him that is near, saith the Lord; and I will heal him" (Isaiah 57:19).*

I found out that it isn't enough to speak God's Word once and then forget it. We must continue speaking it:

> *"Let us hold fast the profession of our faith without wavering; for he is faithful that promised" (Hebrews 10:23).*

When I first saw the importance of continually confessing my faith, I had an immediate opportunity to test my new knowledge. I had been invited to speak at a church in Rockford, Illinois and had recently become on fire with Psalm 5:12, *"For thou, Lord, wilt bless the righteous; with favour wilt thou compass him as with a shield.''*

I began confessing God's favor in advance over the services in Rockford. I said, "I have favor with the pastor, the congregation, and the whole town! Although I could hardly wait to see the results of such favor, the results were not what I had expected.

Church attendance in Rockford wasn't bad, but the people seemed stone cold. They didn't appear to receive the Word at all! Even the pastor didn't seem very friendly. The devil told me, "Don't confess that scripture anymore. It works in reverse!" After the services came to an end, the pastor's wife drove me to the airport. She said, "These services have certainly been...interesting."

I really wanted to give up my profession of faith, but on the plane I said, "The Lord surrounds me with favor as a shield." When I walked into my office, I wanted to tell my secretary everything that had happened. But when she asked about the services I told her, "I had favor as a shield in Rockford, Illinois."

I confessed Psalm 5:12 for the next two weeks! Jesus was the high priest of my profession regardless of how I felt. Then one morning the pastor from the church in Rockford called me. He said, "The congregation didn't seem to respond to your services. I don't understand what has happened, but now the people in my church are banging my door down for your teaching tapes. Will you send us two big boxes of them?"

If I had looked at natural circumstances, I would have given up! "What's the use? It doesn't help to confess the Word, so why try?" **Don't** look at circumstances. Hold fast to your profession of faith and allow your tongue to direct you safely to your ultimate goal. Speak what

God's Word says about your situation.

I've seen people's personalities totally transformed by their speaking God's Word. I remember one woman in our church whose disposition was consistently negative. Our church is called "Happy Church," so my husband would tell me, "She's bad advertising for this church." We could always count on her to have a bad report. If we said, "It's a beautiful evening," she would answer, "You wouldn't say that if you had heard the weather forecast. It's supposed to snow."

Then when the Lord spoke to me about memorizing the book of Proverbs, He told me to ask this negative woman to be my memory partner. I said, "Oh, God. Not her!" But in obedience I called her. I thought, "She'll say no." However, she said, "Yes, I'll be your memory partner."

On the first morning that I called the woman to go over our memory verses, she started complaining: "I am having a terrible day. If you had to live with my husband, you would die!" She would have complained forever, but I stopped her, "I have to take my children to school, so let's hurry." This pattern continued for seven or eight days. Then there was a dramatic change.

I'll never forget the morning I called that woman, bracing myself for her usual complaints. She actually sounded cheery on the telephone! She asked me, "Did you see what was in this verse? Wow, did I get a dynamite revelation!"

That woman's personality changed from being sour and negative to sweet and cheerful. At church she looked happy, and people actually began enjoying her company. One day my husband asked me, "What hap-

How To Be A Mature Christian

pened to her? She is so positive now." What did happen? God's Word coming out of her mouth transformed the woman's attitude. God's Word was a tree of life to her.

The woman could have tried to change her own personality. But in our own natural ability, we cannot change ourselves. The problem was not the woman's personality, but it was a lack of God's Word in her heart. Her bad disposition was just a symptom of the problem. God does not want us to struggle with symptoms; He wants us to bring His Word into the problem for a miracle. God's Word will always turn your sorest defeats into your most shining victories.

Victory in Your Mouth

After Moses died, Joshua led all Israel to victory with the power of God's Word. The Israelites had been wandering in the wilderness for 40 years. An entire generation of unbelieving people had to die before God could lead His chosen people into the land of promise. After Moses died, Joshua shouldered tremendous responsibility.

No sooner than the Israelites crossed the Jordan River, God stopped providing them with manna and water. Shoes and clothing had been supernaturally preserved for 40 years, but no more. The pillar of fire by night and the pillar of cloud by day, which had led the Israelites, disappeared. Joshua had to trust God for food, water, clothing, military protection, and spiritual guidance for over one-million people. Once I was reading about Joshua and the Lord said, "You get nervous about cooking dinner for 10 people. What if you were responsible for one-million?"

Joshua had begun what would be the greatest challenge of his life. That's when God told him, "Meditate on My Word day and night."

"With my schedule?"

God knew that Joshua would need the Word in order to handle such responsibility. He would not take the Promised Land by the power of human strength; He would take it by the supernatural power of the Word:

> *"This book of the law* shall not depart out of thy mouth; *but thou shalt meditate therein day and night, that thou mayest observe to do according to all that is written therein: for then thou shalt make thy way prosperous, and then thou shalt have good success" (Joshua 1:8).*

The Word of God in your mouth determines your success! In the last chapter you saw that Joshua never fought a battle to obtain the Promised Land. If you are fighting and struggling with impossible circumstances, try speaking God's Word instead:

> *"If ye have faith as a grain of mustard seed, ye shall* say unto this mountain, *Remove hence to yonder place; and it shall remove; and nothing shall be impossible unto you" (Matthew 17:20b).*

You don't kick the mountain, and you don't push the mountain. You don't put dynamite under the mountain. Jesus said, "You speak to the mountain." The tongue is what overcomes contrary forces. When Joshua and his men took control of the Promised Land, what did they do? Did they kick the walls? No, they **shouted,** and those walls fell down. How will you knock over the walls of impossiblity in your life? With your tongue! Your tongue casts down mountains and takes you into every promise of God.

After securing victory in the Promised Land, Joshua won yet another battle with the power of his words. Led by Joshua, the Israelites fought against the Amorites. As the battle grew heated, however, nightfall approached. Without light, the Israelites would surely be defeated.

"Then spoke Joshua to the Lord in the day when the Lord delivered up the Amorites before the children of Israel, and he said in the sight of Israel, Sun, stand thou still upon Gibeon; and thou, Moon, in the valley of Ajalon" (Joshua 10:12).

Proverbs 12:6b says, *"The mouth of the upright shall deliver them."* Joshua delivered his people from defeat and death by speaking words of faith. Israel was spared in battle because their leader, Joshua, knew how to abide in the presence and power of God's Word. Even the sun stood still! Your dedication to the truth has the power to save lives around you, too.

At the end of Joshua's life, he was still speaking words of power. When the Israelites settled the Promised Land, Joshua was 86 years old. He could have said, "I'm old and weak. Just give me a tent." But he said, "Give me the mountain with a city on it." He didn't ask for tents, he asked for mountains!

As for Joshua's family, they were all godly people. In Joshua 24:15b, he said, *"As for me and my house, we will serve the Lord."* Joshua believed God for good things, and he spoke his convictions aloud. Like Joshua, you set the course of your destiny with the words you speak.

No other person can speak your words of faith. Jesus said, "**You** speak to the mountain. Job 22:28 says, *"Thou shalt also decree a thing, and it shall be established unto thee: and the light shall shine upon thy ways. "* **You** decree that the mountains will be removed. **You** decree success. Then it shall be established. "Shall," means "future," so sometimes you have to hold fast to your profession of faith.

God's truth contains the supernatural power to conform your life to His perfect will. As you speak His Word, you also bring others in line with God's will. You may have thought, "I can't change another person's life." But God can! I will never believe that our professions of faith do not alter the wills of others. I fought for years against the baptism of the Holy Spirit. But one day I received that baptism because my own mother's prayers and words of faith changed my will and put the call of God on my life. Her words brought heaven to earth for me, and yours can do the same for others.

What about words spoken to harm us? Isaiah 54:17 declares, *"No weapon that is formed against thee shall prosper; and every tongue that shall rise against thee in judgment thou shalt condemn. "* I speak that verse every day.

Bad news travels fast, but so does good news! Dedicate your mouth to the good news of God's Word. Your words work as no other thing to *"make you perfect in every good work to do His will"* (Hebrews 13:21a).

Six Confessions
To Start Your Day

When everything around you starts to look crazy, that's the time for you to stop whatever you're doing and speak God's Word to bring your circumstances back into perspective. I recommend that you start your day with the following six confessions. Set the course of your day with God's Word. I would not start my day without the following faith confessions; I hope they are as special to you as they are to me.

1. Jesus is the Lord over my day.

He's Lord over your day and your disposition! You may wake up in a bad mood. You may find that everyone around you is negative. That's when you need to remember that Jesus is still Lord. He's still on the throne, and He wants to bring life into your day.

2. I'm a new creation in Christ.

You're born again with a new spirit, a new nature, and a new thought life. You were created to be the righteousness of God in Christ Jesus. He is completing you in His image day by day. Don't let satan drag you into the ways of your old nature. Keep your nature in Christ in ascendency by speaking who you are in Him.

3. I cast my cares on the Lord.

Leave yesterday's worries with yesterday. (You're not supposed to be carrying them anyway!) Start your day by giving every worry and care to the Lord. His yoke is easy and His burden is light. Once you give the Lord your cares, don't forget to leave them there.

4. I shall not want.

The Lord is your good shepherd, and you shall not want for any good thing, whether it be spiritual, physical, or material. God is your Jehovah Jireh; He has already seen ahead to meet your needs.

5. He bore my sicknesses, my griefs, and my sorrows.

Jesus took all of these on Himself at the cross. You can't change your own sickness and sorrow. Only the Lord can change them. But you'll see things change when you speak God's Word!

6. I have the mind of Christ.

When you determine to speak God's Word in faith, the Holy Spirit will quicken scriptures to your remembrance. Each day, confess that you have the mind of the Lord. Then expect Him to work with your thoughts. Like Daniel and the three Hebrew children, you can be 10 times wiser than those around you.

Chapter Three

PART III
SPEAK WORDS
THAT BRING PEACE

We all want to have a spirit of faith working in our lives. Faith is simply believing in God's Word and acting on what it says. The Bible says that if you believe God, you will speak what you believe:

> *"We having the same spirit of faith, according as it is written, I believed, and therefore I have spoken; we also believe, and therefore speak"* *(2 Corinthians 4:13).*

A centurion came to Jesus and said, *"I am not worthy that thou shouldest come under my roof: but* speak the word only, *and my servant shall be healed"* (Matthew 8:8). Did the servant receive healing? Yes! Jesus said about the centurion, "His faith is the greatest in all Israel." If you want Jesus to say that your faith is great, then like the centurion you will release faith with your tongue.

A woman who was diseased with an issue of blood received her healing by speaking these faith-filled words:

"For she said, If I may touch but his clothes, I shall be whole" (Mark 5:28).

The Greek tense for "she said" means "she kept saying." The woman continually said, "If I can touch the Lord's clothes I will be healed," and God created the fruit of her lips.

There is another type of confession that is just as important as confessing God's Word. It is the confession of sin:

"He that covereth his sins shall not prosper: but whoso confesseth and forsaketh them shall have mercy" (Proverbs 28:13).

Repentance is the forsaking of sin. But before repentance must come confession. When we confess our sins, God is faithful and just to forgive us **and** cleanse us from all unrighteousness. He not only cleanses us from the sin, but He also cleanses us from the desire to sin. I saw this proved powerfully by an incident that happened in our church.

A man in our congregation deeply loved the Lord, and his ministry was in counseling. He loved to counsel! If it had been possible, that man would have counseled people for 24 hours each day. Once, my husband had to take him aside and say, "You're overdoing the counseling. You need to spend more time with your family."

One day a woman (not from our congregation) called my husband, demanding to talk with him about the man who worked as a counselor. She came to the church and handed my husband some letters that were allegedly written by this counselor. They were love letters.

My husband and I called the man into our office with his wife. Of course, he hotly denied having written the letters. His wife was also very defensive. She said, "My husband would never write such letters! You just do not understand counseling."

We told the woman, "Read the letters for yourself and then decide whether you think they were innocently written." The man had not known we had the letters. He thought the woman had only called us. His wife read the letters and was shattered by what she read.

You might say, "That was cruel." It was not cruel if you understand the outcome.

The man began to cry and carry on: "You don't understand. The letters weren't meant to sound that way. You just want to hurt me."

My husband said plainly, "We do not want to hurt you. We want you to confess your sin and repent so that you will have cleansing. If you cover your sins, you will not receive mercy."

You see, that man was not involved in an affair, but he had taken the first step toward having one. Unless he confessed his sin and repented, the sin would catch up with him and eventually break apart his home.

The man still refused to confess his sin, so my husband walked over to the man, pounded his chair with a fist, and said, **"Repent."**

"Nobody likes me," cried the counselor. "Everyone is so mean to me."

Then my husband boomed, **"Repent!"** The man collapsed sobbing into his wife's lap and said, "I repent."

Today he is being beautifully used by God in the full-time ministry. How did he become free and have this victory? By the power of confessing his sin.

You overcome sin and oppression by the power of what you say. Romans 3:4 says, *"That thou mightest be justified in thy sayings, and mightest overcome when thou art judged."*

Years ago, when I knew very little about confession, I would helplessly watch my husband struggle with deep depression. For all of his life, my husband's brothers and sisters had said, "You'll never amount to anything." He had believed their words and taken them into his life. When depression hit, my husband would hardly talk for days. When he talked, he would speak words of defeat: "I'm no good. I've always been a failure."

One night when in a terrible state of depression, my husband could not sleep. He climbed out of bed, walked to the bedroom window, and stared outside. Depressed! I was so upset by his behavior that I went to another room and prayed in the Spirit for an hour.

When I returned to our room, my husband was still staring silently out the window. I asked him, "Wally, are you a Christian?"

No response. I persisted, "Wally, are you a Christian?"

"You know I am," he retorted.

I said, "If you're a Christian, then you have world-over-coming faith residing on the inside of your spirit."

"Well, I don't!"

"Wally, do you believe that the Bible is God's Word?"

No answer. When I asked again Wally said, "Marilyn, go away and leave me alone."

I insisted, "I won't leave until you answer me! Do you believe that the Bible is God's Word?"

"Yes."

"Then do you have that faith or not? Answer me."

"Yes!" My husband began speaking God's Word. Then he ended up laughing, went to bed, and slept soundly. He never struggled with depression again. He had overcome the enemy with the power of his tongue.

"The word of God abideth in you, and ye have overcome the wicked one" (1 John 2:14).

God's Word abides in you, and when you speak it, satan must flee. Demons had to obey Jesus when He spoke God's Word. When He cast out devils, they had no choice but to leave.

"Yes, but that was Jesus." Wait a minute! The seven sons of Sceva tried to cast out demons "in the name of Jesus whom Paul preaches." The demons said, "We know Jesus, and we also know Paul." And if you're a child of God, demons know **you**! They have to flee when you speak God's Word in the name of Jesus. I once heard a man say, "You can't out-think a demon, but you can out-talk one." You out-talk demons with God's Word.

"Concerning the works of men, by the word of thy lips I have kept me from the paths of the destroyer" (Psalm 17:4).

Sow Righteousness

A mature Christian uses his tongue to sow the fruit of righteousness in his life. God's Word is for you to sow in every possible opportunity:

"But the wisdom that is from above is first pure, and then peaceable,..." (James 3:17a).

God's Word is pure. It does not set the standard for purity—it is purity. Because God's Word is pure, it is also peaceful.

"gentle, and easy to be entreated,..." (James 3:17b).

God's wisdom is easy to entreat. God does not try to hide His Word from us. In James chapter one, James said, "If you need God's wisdom, just ask for it."

"Full of mercy and good fruits, without partiality, and without hypocrisy" (James 3:17c).

God's Word is full of mercy and brings victory for all! When James spoke against respecters of persons he said, "Mercy rejoices against judgment." God's Word is not partial. It is not hypocritical. God's Word does not choose or prefer one person above another. It is full of mercy for **everyone.**

"And the fruit of righteousness is sown in peace of them that make peace" (James 3:18).

Do your words bring peace and victory to others? Do they bring peace and victory to yourself? They will if you speak God's Word. If you want to sow the fruit of righteousness in abundance: speak God's Word.

Chapter Four

WALK IN GOD'S GRACE

Read any newspaper from front to back and you'll find in-depth descriptions of all kinds of fights and wars. Whether on an international scope or a personal level, wars are nothing new.

Did anyone teach us how to quarrel? No! James said, *"The spirit that dwelleth in us lusteth to envy"* (James 4:5). To the spirit of man, conflict is a natural part of everyday life. It really gets hot sometimes. One of the most shocking things a baby Christian learns is that even other Christians aren't perfect. How do you deal with those relationships? Even though we may be surrounded by fights and struggles, Christians can overcome the spirit of war by the power of the Spirit of God. James reveals how we can be mature Christians by putting down conflicts, rising into faith, and experiencing God's grace.

What is the root of warring? It is selfishness, the basis for all sin. Remember, satan first sinned by trying to exalt himself above God. Sin is the same today. People say, "I want **my** way, regardless of the cost."

"From whence come wars and fightings among you? come they not hence, even of your lusts that war in your members?" (James 4:1).

Wars are in our members, therefore they take place in the realm of our senses. We see something or hear something, we get offended, and soon we are at war against someone:

"Ye lust, and have not: ye kill, and desire to have, and cannot obtain: ye fight and war, yet ye have not, because ye ask not" (James 4:2).

It is disturbing to know that Christians are fighting among themselves. It is even more disturbing to know that the reason these conflicts take place is because of envy. People are striving in competition against each other, jealous of each other's gains. Why? Because their eyes are not on God. Those whose eyes are on material possessions instead of God will find that their prayers go unanswered. Even if they ask God for something, their motives are selfish: "I want the new car because so-and-so has one."

"Ye ask and receive not, because ye ask amiss, that ye may consume it upon your lusts" (James 4:3).

God wants to meet all our needs, but He cannot do so when **things** are more important to us than He is. Jesus said, "You cannot serve two masters." To befriend the world and its material benefits is to turn from God:

"Ye adulterers and adulteresses, know ye not that the friendship of the world is enmity with God? whosoever therefore will be a friend of the world is the enemy of God" (James 4:4).

James is not talking about physical adultery; he is saying, "Sin is spiritual adultery." We cannot love the world and love God at the same time. The world's love puts self first, but God's love puts others first. The world's love will pass away, but God's love is eternal:

"Love not the world, neither the things that are in the world. If any man love the world, the love of the Father is not in him. And the world passeth away and the lusts thereof, but he that doeth the will of God abideth forever" (1 John 2:15-17).

If you look to what the world can offer you, you are befriending the world. That friendship brings selfishness, while God calls His people to selflessness. James said, "The world's love opposes God." You might think, "I'm fighting for myself." But James says of such a fight, "You are fighting with God." Don't fight with God by befriending the world and its gains, because God always wins.

Be the Image of Christ

You might say, "I can't change." But God can change you! He has a simple solution to focus your eyes on Him:

"And be not conformed to this world: but be ye transformed by the renewing of your mind, that ye may prove what is that good, and acceptable, and perfect, will of God" (Romans 12:2).

As you renew your mind to God's Word, your personality and desires conform to the image of Christ in you. I understand that a seed, when split in half, bears the image of what it will be at maturity. The seed of God's Word in you has the full potential to mature you into Christ's image. You develop that maturity by renewing your mind to God's Word. But unless you read the Word, you cannot reach your full potential in Christ.

I have watched what happens to those who neglect God's Word, and it grieves me. A man and his whole family were saved, baptized, and Spirit-filled at our church. They never missed a service, but I knew that the father struggled with reading his Bible. Then one day he became offended by another church member, so he and his family left the church permanently.

After leaving the church, the man became involved in drinking, taking drugs, and he was unfaithful to his wife. The marriage and family broke apart. Although the man's family still serves the Lord, his tragedy could have been avoided if he had disciplined himself to renew his mind with God's Word.

People get saved and think, "Hurray! Everything is marvelous." But if they don't stay involved with reading God's Word, everything won't be marvelous. Fights and wars will come, and they will be victims or victors, depending on their use of the Word.

In the long run, consistent Bible reading pays off. You can be saved, Spirit-filled, and in church every day, but only God's Word will renew your mind. Only God's Word will keep you walking in spiritual discernment and out of sense knowledge.

Why does the devil bring so much strife to the church? He wants to bring disharmony because it quenches the flow of God's power. The enemy wants to divide Christians and cause them to argue among themselves about issues such as healing, or speaking in tongues. But if we are in division, our eyes are not on God.

I have thought many times about Dr. Cho's church in Seoul, Korea. His church is the largest in the world. This church is influencing its nation because so many people are in agreement. Politicians want to speak there because they know that the members could easily get them elected. That church has power and authority because its members are of one mind.

Psalm 133:1 says, *"Behold, how good and pleasant it is for brethren to dwell together in unity."* It's not just good and pleasant to dwell in unity—it's powerful!

Abraham had a perfect opportunity to quarrel with his nephew, Lot. Their herds had grown so large that there was a shortage of grazing land. The two men would have to divide their herds into different areas. Abraham told Lot, "There are two areas—a well-watered plain and a mountainous region. Choose the land you prefer."

Abraham could have dictated to Lot the land he should choose. But Abraham did not have to compete with Lot to obtain the choicest land. He knew that no matter where he lived, God would cause him to prosper. Lot chose the well-watered plain for himself, leaving the arid, mountainous region to his uncle. Poor choice. Because Lot walked by sense knowledge he didn't prosper, but Abraham did. You see, faith, not sense knowledge will bring you out on top.

What if Abraham had taken offense at Lot? He could have complained, "I've raised Lot as my own son, and look at how he has treated me. I have to live alone on a dry, desolate mountain." Some other person would have picked up Abraham's offense and passed it on: "Did you hear about what Lot did to Abraham?" Then the person would excuse his gossip by saying, "It's a matter of prayer."

By the time Lot would have come on the scene, nobody would have been talking to him. They would have been thinking, "That thug! How could he be so thoughtless?"

When two people begin to fight and others pick up their offenses, a fight becomes a full-fledged war. Christians will never win by picking up each other's offenses! We as Christians must stop sharing our offenses with others and instead go to the Lord in prayer. Only then will we stop disunity and open ourselves to the flow of God's power.

Living in the sense realm brings trouble because it causes us to walk by sight instead of by faith. I like the way James doesn't just say, "Be mature!" and hit you over the head: "Clean up your act!" He shows us how to rise above wars into faith:

"But he giveth more grace. Wherefore he saith, God resisteth the proud, but giveth grace unto the humble" (James 4:6).

You say, "I can't help but fight with others." But God wants to give you **grace.** People have called grace, "God's unmerited favor." But it is more than that. Grace is God's supernatural power wrought on your behalf. When satan, the whole world, and your flesh are coming against you, God has even **more** grace to make you a winner in your situation.

James said that grace is for the humble. Being humble does not mean that you lie down on the ground and wait for people to walk on you. It means that you yield yourself in total dependence on God. Don't say, "What about the other person's sin?" Who is right or wrong does not matter! Leave the other person's sin with God, and let Him deal with it. Just take care of yourself. It's your own relationship with God that is important. How can you humble yourself? James tells you:

"Submit yourselves therefore to God. Resist the devil, and he will flee from you. Draw nigh to God, and he will draw nigh to you. Cleanse your hands, ye sinners; and purify your hearts, ye double minded" (James 4:7,8).

Step one is always to submit yourself to God. No matter how vindicated you feel in your anger toward another person, submit yourself to God. No matter how impossible a situation may appear to be, submit yourself to God.

Years ago a young man in our church was experiencing major problems with drug abuse. He was in and out of church all the time. He would leave his wife and children for months, and then he would come back and say, "I'm resisting the devil." But you'll never resist the devil until you first submit to God. If your prayer life and Bible reading are inconsistent, you are not submitted to God. How can you resist the enemy if you are fighting with God Himself?

James said, "First submit. Then you have put yourself in a position to resist, and the devil **must** flee." Then James gave you another tip: "Draw near to God, and He will draw near to you."

The major goal in every Christian's life should be to know the Lord better every day. When we try to manipulate our own circumstances, we create distance between ourselves and God. Instead, draw near to Him. Stop warring and let Him battle for you.

We always want to clean up somebody else's life, but James charges us, *"Cleanse* your *hands, ye sinners; and purify* your *hearts, ye double minded"* (James 4:8b). We are double-minded when we try to walk by faith, and at the same time, live in sense knowledge. We purify ourselves from a double mind by submitting our wills to God, resisting the devil, and drawing as close as possible to God.

James said about a double-minded man, "He shall receive nothing from God." But when we purify our hearts with the single motive of walking close to the Lord, we are in a position to receive from Him because we no longer have selfish motives.

"Be afflicted, and mourn, and weep: let your laughter be turned to mourning, and your joy to heaviness" (James 4:9).

Someone who is trying to please God and the world at the same time is the most miserable person you will ever see. God is saying, "Don't ignore the sin. Get down to business and repent." Why? Because then you are in a position to receive grace (supernatural strength) from God. God always wants us to win, and can help us to do so when we submit ourselves to Him:

"Humble yourselves in the sight of the Lord, and he shall lift you up" (James 4:10).

If you are depending on your own strength in a trial, then God cannot use His strength to help you. Many years ago, someone told me, "As pastors, you and your husband should never tell people that you have problems. Handle problems by yourselves because, as far as others are concerned, you shouldn't have problems." Then we experienced a major trial involving our son, and what did we do? We told the church. They loved us, prayed for us, and provided a tremendous support system in our crisis. It's a mistake when the church thinks that its leadership doesn't have problems. Whether you are in full-time ministry, or are a lay person, don't be too proud to obtain the support of other members of the Body. Never be too proud in a trial to say, "I can't handle this problem myself." When you are your weakest, the Lord will deliver you with His own strength.

You might say, "But people will criticize." So what's new? Criticism is nothing new; we'll always have it! The important thing is that we please the Lord by agreeing with others on His Word. Be honest, and if you need help don't run from God—run **to** Him. Let Him fight your wars because He has already won them for you in Christ.

As you rely increasingly on God's grace, conflicts will prove to be less of a snare to you. Then in order to move in God's perfect will for your life, believe and act on God's Word:

"Go to now, ye that say, To day or to morrow we will go into such a city, and continue there a year, and buy and sell, and get gain: Whereas ye know not what shall be on the morrow. For what is your life? It is even a vapour, that appeareth for a little time, and then vanisheth away. For that ye ought to say, If the Lord will, we shall live, and do this, or that. But now ye rejoice in all

your boastings: all such rejoicing is evil" (James 4:13-16).

What does it mean to rejoice in your boastings? It means that your eyes are fixed on accomplishments and plans, rather than on God. You're worried about your own goals, not God's goals for you. Our lives are so short that if we expect to accomplish the Lord's will, we must allow Him total control. Don't plan ahead without knowing God's will. Our lives are now God's responsibility; our part is simply to allow God to stay in control. When we let Him handle our problems, he'll do the supernatural.

Yielded to Rest

When you know that the Lord has prepared your way, no person or circumstances will rattle you. You can stop every war, whether it is within or without, by completely yielding yourself to God's will. In yieldedness you find rest:

"Let us labour therefore to enter into that rest, lest any man fall after the same example of unbelief" (Hebrews 3:10).

A woman I know was saved shortly after her husband's death, when her children were all in their twenties. The devil told her, "If you had been saved earlier, your children would not be so wild." Her children were all taking drugs, and their mother was tormented with fear because they were all unsaved.

Then one night as the woman was praying, God spoke to her and said, "Leave your children with Me. It is My will to save them, so stop harrassing yourself." From that night on, the children's mother never worried about them. She never cooked up schemes to get them saved.

She just said, "They are God's problem. He will send the laborers."

One morning at four o'clock, the mother was startled from sleep by a telephone call. It was her son, who said, "I have heard the voice of God. What should I do?" The boy's mother led him to the Lord. He was Spirit-filled, attended Bible college, and became an assistant pastor in Tulsa, Oklahoma. Today that man directs a large youth ministry. Every member of his family is saved because his mother decided to allow God to perform His will by leaving her struggles with Him.

You will never win a war through the ability of your own flesh. It is through entering into God's grace and trusting Him for victory that you win every time. Now repent of any warring that you may have been involved in. Have you fought for a job? Quarreled with a spouse or a member of your church? Struggled with a war of condemnation? Your Father is a God of peace. Commit yourself to rest in His perfect will by faith, and He will grant you grace that vanquishes wars and makes you walk in the high places of peace.

Chapter Five

SPEND WISELY, PRAY FERVENTLY

The Lord is very aware of two elements of your life: your giving and your prayers. It is interesting that, as described in the book of Acts, it was the prayer life and sowing of alms that brought Cornelius to the Lord's attention. Throughout the Bible, financial giving and commitment to prayer have distinguished the mature men of God. It is no surprise, then, that James ended his epistle on the subjects of money and prayer.

Money

When Jesus sat near the treasury in the temple, He did more than just sit there—He watched what people gave. Had we been there, probably we would have averted our eyes from the treasury and politely looked in another direction. But the Lord watched and noticed people's giving then, and He still notices it today.

Sometimes when ministers talk about money, people become very sensitive. They say, "It's a personal matter." While our giving **should** be a personal matter between ourselves and God, it is very important that we give. In fact, the Lord is not only aware of His children's finances; He is also aware of the finances of the wicked:

> *"Go to now, ye rich men, weep and howl for your miseries that shall come upon you. Your riches are corrupted, and your garments are motheaten. Your gold and silver is cankered; and the rust of them shall be a witness against you, and shall eat your flesh as it were fire. Ye have heaped treasure together for the last days. Behold the hire of the labourers who have reaped down your fields, which is of you kept back by fraud, crieth: and the cries of them which have reaped are entered into the ears of the Lord of sabaoth" (James 5:1-4).*

Who is talking against the rich men? The cries of God's people have brought a serious matter to His attention. The wages that were held back from the laborers are also crying out! Not only have laborers been cheated of the wages due them, but the deceitful employers have misspent the money by nourishing only their personal desires:

> *"Ye have lived in pleasure on the earth, and been wanton; ye have nourished your hearts, as in a day of slaughter. Ye have condemned and killed the just; and he doth not resist you" (James 5:5,6.*

The key phrase for the final chapter of James is, *"Ye have heaped treasure together for the last days"* (James 5:3). Why would an unbeliever store up treasure for the last days? He wouldn't! God is saying that the rich ungodly people whose fortunes have been amassed for their own lusts will lose their treasure in the last days. James said, *"Weep and howl."* Why would a rich man weep over his money? He would only weep over **losing** it. Proverbs 13:22 says, *"The wealth of the sinner is laid up for the just."* James 5 reveals the same thing. In the last days, God will take wealth from wicked men and give it to His people. This truth is found throughout the Old Testament:

"For God giveth to a man that is good in his sight wisdom, and knowledge, and joy: but to the sinner he giveth travail, to gather and to help up, that he may give to him that is good before God" (Ecclesiastes 2:26).

The Lord has given some ungodly men the ability to acquire wealth. But the righteous ones will eventually inherit that wealth:

"Though he heap up silver as the dust, and prepare raiment as the clay; He may prepare it, but the just shall put it on, and the innocent shall divide the silver" (Job 27:16).

Sometimes we observe those around us and see that some very evil men possess huge fortunes. But God doesn't want us to worry about them. In Proverbs 24:19,20 He said, *"Fret not thyself because of evil men, neither be thou envious at the wicked; For there shall be no reward to the evil man; the candle of the wicked shall be put out."*

God's plan for His people was never that we store up riches. His plan has always been for us to give freely of our resources to the work of His kingdom. By doing so, we open the doors for God to bless us again. Don't worry about how other people gain their prosperity. Just look to God as your source, not to men. All of the riches that this world can offer belong to the Lord and are for His people:

"And I will shake all nations, and the desire of all nations shall come: And I will fill this house with glory, saith the Lord of hosts. The silver is mine, and the gold is mine, saith the Lord" (Haggai 2:7,8).

If the silver and gold all belong to God, then why is it in the possession of evil men? Because they will use their ability to benefit the kingdom of God, without even knowing it. Their money will be used to accomplish a quick work of spreading the gospel. Haggai continued:

"The glory of this latter house shall be greater than that of the former, saith the Lord of hosts: and in this place will I give peace, saith the Lord of hosts" (Haggai 2:9).

The former and latter houses in this scripture are symbolic of the Old and New Testament churches. The New Testament Church will be greater than the Old Testament Church. Why? Because God will bring the latter house into the gold and silver. Many people fail to realize that it takes money to bring the gospel to others. But whether you like it or not, covering the earth with God's Word is very expensive.

In the 1940's tremendous revival swept the church, but this revival only prepared the way for what is yet to come. Had silver and gold been poured into the church's work, the churches would still have lacked the technological resources necessary to minister the gospel throughout the world. At that time, use of the radio medium was still limited, and there was no television. Today we have radio, television, video, and even satellite. All of these are excellent tools with which to communicate God's Word in other countries.

Through video, the Word is reaching formerly inaccessible countries with outstanding results. Some missionaries receive their personal teachings and edification from video cassettes. All of these valuable means to share the gospel cost a great deal of money. But we don't have to worry about where the money will come from, for God has said, "The silver and gold are Mine."

In the end times, wicked men will suffer the loss of their riches to God's people. This wealth will not be dispensed to people who say, "The wealth of the wicked is laid up for me!" The wealth will be for those who will return it to the unsaved in the form of the gospel! This is not a new idea. In the earliest Old Testament times, God often applied the finances of heathen men to His own causes.

When the Israelites departed from Egypt under the leadership of Moses, God moved on the hearts of the Egyptians to provide the Israelites with much wealth. Only God could have caused such a thing! To understand the quality of the wealth received by the Israelites, it helps to consider examples of Egyptian artifacts recovered from tombs. The riches from those tombs are some of the finest in the world. Those people were wealthy. Just imagine what the Israelites took with them—what God gave them—when they left Egypt! The Egyptians had forced God's people to work as slaves, and for years they had been unpaid. But God heard their cries, and He saw that they collected their deserved wages. God paid His people with the funds of wicked men. They had gold, rubies, diamonds—even linen with which to build their temple.

Years later, the Israelites were in another captivity, this time in Babylon. The Jewish temple had been destroyed by Nebuchadnezzar's armies, and its goods had been stolen. But God stirred the heart of a heathen king named Cyrus to let the Israelites go free. Cyrus was so moved by the power of God's Word that when he released the Israelites, he restored to them the wealth stolen from their temple, and presented them with tons of riches from his own country's treasury. The Israelites returned to their homeland, Jerusalem, with abundance bestowed on them by a heathen king.

The examples of the Egyptian and Babylonian captivities have one thing in common. Each time the Israelites received money from the wicked, it was to be used to build the Lord's house. Today, heathen wealth is still appointed for the building of a temple: a temple constructed from living stones! When God secures money from the wicked, it is to be used for building the Body of Christ.

Some people say, "I'm a Christian, but I am not prosperous." The rules for obtaining prosperity are in God's Word. God told Joshua, "Keep My Word in your mouth, and don't let it depart from before your eyes, if you want to be successful." To prosper, our first priority should be God's priority: His Word.

"Receive, I pray thee, the law from his mouth, and lay up his words in thine heart. If thou return to the Almighty, thou shalt build up, thou

shalt put iniquity far from thy tabernacles (Job 22:22,23).

If you've blown it somewhere, if you're in strife with someone, or if you haven't been trusting God, return to Him. Put iniquity far from your tabernacle. The Hebrew for "Almighty" is *El Shaddai,* meaning, "the God who is more than enough." El Shaddai means that God builds, adds, and increases His abundance in your life. This is the God who takes your circumstances far beyond your dreams.

In Job 22, the scripture says, *"Put sin far from your tabernacle."* **You** are the temple of God. Dedicate yourself to Him as an instrument of righteousness. If you lack prosperity, ask the Holy Spirit to show you why. The enemy could be stealing from you, but sometimes we miss God's blessing just by being impractical.

A mother of two teenage daughters once told me, "I can no longer afford to send my daughters to Christian school." I asked the woman about her employment, and discovered that she only worked three days each week. She had never even thought about working a five-day week. I suggested that her girls might further appreciate their schooling if they worked part-time to help pay for their education. You see, there was an area of impracticality in this woman's life that prevented her from enjoying prosperity.

Other likely sources of lack include strife and failure to tithe. James said, "Where strife is, you find confusion and every kind of evil." God has commanded us to pay our tithes. Every guideline in God's Word has been included for one reason: so that He can bless us. But we must observe God's rules if we desire to receive His benefits:

> *"Then shalt thou lay up gold as dust, and the gold of Ophir as the stones of the brooks. Yea, the Almighty shall be thy defense, and thou shalt have plenty of silver. For then shalt thou have thy delight in the Almighty, and shalt lift up thy face unto God" (Job 22:24-26).*

The gold of Ophir and the silver represent material wealth. But spiritual wealth is also contained in this scripture, as Job has said, *"Then shalt thou have thy delight in the Almighty"* (Job 22:26). God wants your entire being to prosper. 3 John 2 says, *"Behold, I wish above all things that thou mayest prosper and be in health,* even as thy soul prospereth." You can enjoy the Lord's prosperity when they your trust is in Him.

James knew that it was God's will to bless you, and he knew that God would use the finances of the heathen. But, like growing into Christian maturity, receiving the prosperity of the Lord can take time. James recognized that you may have to hold fast to patience in order to receive from God:

> *"Be patient, therefore, brethren, unto the coming of the Lord. Behold, the husbandman waiteth for the precious fruit of the earth, and hath long patience for it, until he receive the early and latter rain" (James 5:7).*

To be patient does not mean sitting around saying, "One day the Lord will come take us away." Patience is a fruit of the spirit. Like love, it is resident within every believer. All the fruits of the spirit must be exercised by our wills. Working together, they make us **doers** of God's Word. Therefore, patience involves activity.

Through patience, Job gained victory in his trial. Through patience, we will gain victory in our trials:

"Grudge not one against another, brethren, lest ye be condemned: behold, the judge standeth before the door. Take, my brethren, the prophets who have spoken in the name of the Lord, for an example of suffering affliction, and of patience. Behold, we count them happy which endure. Ye have heard of the patience of Job, and have seen the end of the Lord, that the Lord is very pitiful and of tender mercy" (Job 5:10,11).

Don't complain and grumble about tests and trials in your life. James said, "Happy are those who endure." We need to endure our trials in a spirit of faith. Remember that God corrected Jonah for having a wrong attitude, even though he was obedient. Our attitudes will be right if we believe God's Word and say, "Job had a happy ending, and so will I."

Job lived for 69 years before his trial, which only lasted for one year, until he was 70 years old. Most people want to dwell on Job's suffering, but his suffering is not your example. You are to look at the end of Job. After the trial, God returned everything to Job in double portion. He even lived for 70 more years to enjoy the blessings that God gave him. Be patient and trust God that the end of your trial, whether financial or whatever, is tremendous blessing.

Prayer

As I said before, patience involves activity. If there is a waiting period before you receive prosperity, it is essential that you keep your eyes on God. Reading His Word is a part of being patient. The other part of patience is prayer. Prayer should be every Christian's key for patience in hardship:

"Is any among you afflicted? let him pray."
(James 5:13a).

The word *afflicted* does not mean "sick." It means "distressed," or "enduring hardship." If you are in a trial, you **can** do more than just grit your teeth and vow to persevere. Prayer will make your patience work for you. If you go around dwelling on your affliction, you are not in faith.

You are to pray according to God's provision, not according to the problems you are experiencing. You can tell God the problem, but don't dwell on circumstances. Dwell on solutions from His Word. Say, "God, Your Word promises that I will always triumph in Christ."

I am not telling you to deny the existence of problems. Some mental science religions say, "Problems are not there at all." The Lord never denied problems. He said, *"In the world ye shall have tribulation: but be of good cheer; I have overcome the world"* (John 16:33b). If you are in Christ, then you have overcome the world, too. If you are enduring affliction, your prayers bring the promises from God's Word to work in your situation.

To prove that your prayers are very important to God, James gave a shining example from God's Word. He showed you the prophet, Elijah. We think, "Elijah was a great man." But James said that the prophet was *"a man subject to like passions as we are."* Elijah blew it, just like we do, but his prayer life should be an example to us.

"Elias was a man subject to like passions as we

are, and he prayed earnestly that it might not rain: and it rained not on the earth by the space of three years and six months. And he prayed again, and the heaven gave rain, and the earth brought forth her fruit" (James 5:17,18).

When Elijah prayed, the heavens, which had been closed from rain for three years, brought forth rain to water the earth. Today we are awaiting a rain: the latter rain spoken of by James:

"Behold, the husbandman waiteth for the precious fruit of the earth, and hath long patience for it, until he receive the early and latter rain" (James 5:7b).

We have a great hope for this life, and for our futures. After the latter rain, we will have an eternity with the Lord Jesus Christ. That is a victory for which we should praise God every day!

Sometimes it is important that we pray with others in order to see victory:

"Is any sick among you? let him call for the elders of the church; and let them pray over him, anointing with oil in the name of the Lord: And the prayer of faith shall save the sick, and the Lord shall raise him up; and if he have committed sins, they shall be forgiven him" (James 5:14,15).

In this context, what could be **one** reason for a person's sickness? Could sin cause sickness? That is what James has said. But is all sickness caused by sin? No! When you see a sick person, don't think to yourself, "He has sin in his life." You don't know that! Those types of judgments will keep you in sense knowledge instead of spiritual discernment.

The prayer of faith is what will raise the sick person, whether he has sinned or not. Why anoint someone with oil? The prayer, not the oil, will raise him. But for some people, anointing with oil provides their faith with a point of contact. The laying on of hands may provide faith with a point of contact. God gave us many ways to receive healing by faith. But all Christians have a direct line to God through prayer in the name of Jesus.

Let's take the scripture literally. Why should we pray with a church elder? I recommend that you not go to a novice Christian, because he is inexperienced in faith. You should seek a person in leadership who has experience exercising faith for healing, and who knows the power of God's Word.

One woman who attended a very liberal church told me, "I was suffering from asthma, and I read the scripture in James 5:14. I asked my father to call the elders from my church to pray for my healing." Her father, a Pentecostal believer, said, "Honey, if they pray for you, you'll die!" The point is, a person who prays for you should have faith to be able to pray an effectual, fervent prayer.

"Confess your faults one to another, and pray one for another, that ye may be healed. The effectual fervent prayer of a righteous man availeth much" (James 5:16).

When you pray with your church elders, the Holy Spirit may reveal some sin. If so, confess that sin and repent. The scripture does **not** say, "Confess your faults to everyone." It says, "Confess them one to another."

Perhaps you only want to confess your faults to God. However, if you have battled a persistent weakness or temptation, perhaps you should link your faith with that of another believer. Don't go to the whole church. Pick out one person whose life displays the fruit of the spirit, and whom you know to be discreet.

Many people read, "The effectual fervent prayer of a righteous man," and they immediately think, "I'm not righteous." In ourselves, we are not righteous. But we are righteous **in Christ,** because He is righteous. We have been made to be the righteousness of God in Christ Jesus. In the name of Jesus you have righteousness, and therefore your prayers avail much!

Your prayers are so important. They release the flow of the latter rain to spread the gospel worldwide. Your prayers release God's power to bring wealth from the hands of wicked men and pour it into the gospel. Your prayers can save the lives of many.

An important accompaniment to your prayer should be praise. Every day, spend some time thinking about the things for which you can praise God. I have found that the more time I spend in praise, the more I have victories.

"Is any merry? let him sing psalms" (James 5:13b).

Rejoice in the Lord's answers to your small prayers, as well as your big prayers. You can sit in a service and wonder why only 12 people were saved. You can think to yourself, "The organist played the wrong music for this altar call." But if you are encouraging a critical spirit, then you are in unbelief. You close the door to God's miracles with a critical attitude. Of course more people could come forward for any altar call! Of course things could be better. There is never any question that circumstances can improve in church services. But you'll see far more miracles if you purpose to live in an attitude of praise. *"Is any merry? Let him sing psalms."*

James was a pastor with a heart to win souls. His love extended past his church in Jerusalem to cover churches scattered abroad—and is still reaching those churches today. His message is, "Be mature by growing in faith." But most of all, James' message is one of love: for the Lord, for the Body of Christ, and for the souls who will be saved as we become doers of God's Word.

—NOTES—

—NOTES—

—NOTES—

—NOTES—

—NOTES—

Receive Jesus Christ as
Lord and Savior of Your Life

The Bible says, "that if thou shalt confess with thy mouth the Lord Jesus, and shalt believe in thine heart that God hath raised him from the dead, thou shalt be saved. For with the heart man believeth unto righteousness; and with the mouth confession is made unto salvation" (Romans 10:9-10).

To receive Jesus Christ as Lord and Savior of your life, sincerely pray this prayer from your heart:

Dear Jesus,

I believe that You died for me and that You rose again on the third day. I confess to You that I am a sinner and that I need Your love and forgiveness. Come into my life, forgive my sins and give me eternal life. I confess You now as my Lord. Thank You for my salvation!

Signed _____

Date _____

Write to us. We will send you information to help you with your new life in Christ. Marilyn Hickey Ministries • P.O. Box 17340 • Denver, CO 80217

●━●━●━●━●━●━●━●━●━●━●━●━●━●━●━●━●━●━●━●

**Let us join our faith with yours
for your prayer needs. Fill out below
and send to:**

Marilyn Hickey Ministries
P.O. Box 17340
Denver, Colorado 80217

Prayer Request _____

_____

_____

_____

_____

Name ^{Mr. Mrs. Miss} _____

Address _____

State _____ Zip _____

Phone _____

●━●━●━●━●━●━●━●━●━●━●━●━●━●━●━●━●━●━●━●

For Your Information

Free Monthly Magazine

☐ Please send me your free monthly magazine TIME WITH HIM (including daily devotionals, timely articles, and ministry updates!)

Tapes and Books

☐ Please send me Marilyn's latest product catalog.

MARILYN HICKEY PRODUCT CATALOG

Name ^{Miss Mrs. Mr.} _____

PLEASE PRINT

Address _____

City _____

State _____ Zip _____

Phone ( ) _____

Mail to:
Marilyn Hickey Ministries
P.O. Box 17340
Denver, CO 80217

TOUCHING YOU WITH THE LOVE OF JESUS!

24-Hour Counseling and Prayer
LIFELINE

When was the last time that you could say, "He touched me, right where I hurt?" No matter how serious the nature of your call, we're here to listen, offer solutions based upon the Word, and show you how to touch Jesus for real answers to real problems.

**Call us anytime day or night,
and let's touch Jesus, together!**

(303) 777-5029
WE CARE!

BOOKS BY MARILYN HICKEY
ORDER BLANK

BOOK TITLE	CODE	PRICE EACH	QUAN.	TOTAL PRICE
Beat Tension	BK I	$ .75		
Change Your Life	BK V	.75		
Conquering Setbacks	BK C	.75		
Dear Marilyn	BK KK	6.95		
Divorce Is Not The Answer	BK D	2.95		
Egypt Revisited In Prophecy	BK H	1.95		
Experience Long Life	BK Z	.75		
Fasting & Prayer	BK W	.75		
Fear Free, Faith Filled	BK U	3.25		
Freedom From Bondages	BK HH	4.95		
Gift Wrapped Fruit	BK O	2.00		
God IN You, TO You, And FOR You	BK AA	4.95		
God's Benefit: Healing	BK P	.75		
God's Covenant For Your Family	BK S	4.95		
God's RX For A Hurting Heart	BK Q	3.25		
God's Seven Keys To Make You Rich	BK N	.75		
Hold On To Your Dreams	BK Y	.75		
How To Be A Mature Christian	BK II	5.95		
How To Become More Than A Conqueror	BK K	.75		
How To Win Friends	BK J	.75		
I Can Be Born Again	BK EE	.75		
I Can Dare To Be An Achiever	BK FF	.75		
Keys To Healing Rejection	BK M	.75		
Motivational Gifts	BK X	3.50		
#1 Key to Success—Meditation	BK BB	2.50		
Power Of Forgiveness	BK B	.75		
Receive the Evidence of the Spirit-filled Life	BK DD	4.95		
Renew Your Mind	BK E	.75		
Signs in the Heavens	BK GG	4.95		
Smooth Out Your Rough Edges	BK JJ	7.95		
Speak The Word	BK A	.75		
Standing In The Gap	BK L	.75		
Treading With Angels	BK F	2.95		
Winning Over Weight	BK T	.75		
Women Of The Word	BK G	.75		
Your Miracle Source	BK R	2.50		

Prices subject to change without notice

TOTAL

Please Print:

Name Miss Mrs. Mr. _____

Address _____

City _____ State _____ Zip _____

Phone ( ) _____

Circle One:

Please print number   Expiration date

Signature

P.O. Box 17340 • Denver, CO 80217